CW00952494

WAR
IN 100 EVENTS

WAR
IN 100 EVENTS

MARTIN VAN CREVELD

The
History
Press

First published 2017

The History Press
The Mill, Brimscombe Port
Stroud, Gloucestershire, GL5 2QG
www.thehistorypress.co.uk

All illustrations by Martin Latham

Text © Martin van Creveld, 2017
Illustrations © The History Press, 2017

British Library Cataloguing in Publication Data.
A catalogue record for this book is available from the British Library.

ISBN 978 0 7509 8241 2

Typesetting and origination by The History Press
Printed and bound in Great Britain by TJ International Ltd

Contents

Part II. Medieval War, 476–1494 CE

Part III. Fighting with Guns, 1495–1815 CE

Part IV. Industrial War, 1815–1945 CE

Part V. The Regression of War, 1945 CE–Present

Why this Book

As many readers will know, I have spent much of my life studying war. As far as I can reconstruct my career, my interest in it developed in four stages. The first spark was provided by a Dutch schoolbook, *Wereld Geschiendenis in een Notedop* (*World History in a Nutshell*), which had a chapter about the Persian Wars. Here were the Greeks, a small people but brave, making the supreme sacrifice, as Leonidas' Spartans did at Thermopylae. They fought and overcame a much larger, more powerful foe – a theme that has stirred the imagination of countless people aside from myself.

Having studied and mastered my craft, starting in the early 1980s I found myself working for the Pentagon. My mentor there was Andy Marshall, the head of Net Assessment and a man who took a keen interest in all sorts of theoretical problems. My involvement with him caused me to try to understand what the study of military history can teach us in respect to our present-day problems; what lessons one could, and could not, draw from it; how to go about doing so; and so on.

Next, I shifted to the place of war in human affairs in general. After all, war does not on its own stand. Rather, it is inextricably linked to politics, economics, social affairs, culture, religion, and what not. Needless to say, the ties linking all these things are reciprocal. All form part of an infinitely complex net. Nevertheless, I think there is much truth in Leon Trotsky's famous words about war being the locomotive of history. In studying it, my objective was to find out how the locomotive works as well as the way it makes the carriages move.

Finally, I came to look at war in Platonic terms: the way Plato puts it in the introduction to the *Republic*, the ideal city is not meant simply as a political construct. It is that, of course. But it is also a metaphor for the human soul. One that, being written in large characters, is easier than the latter to read and understand. The same, I think, is true of war. The reason why war is such an excellent magnifying glass is because those engaged in it labour under fewer constraints than people in any other activity, if only because participants have nothing to lose so almost everything is permitted. The result is that it brings out the full range of human potential – the good as well as the bad.

As the title of this book suggests, my objective in writing it was to compress the essence of all this into as small and concise a space as I could manage. This is why it focuses on the 100 most important military events; covers events not just in Europe, as is so often the case, but in various other parts of the world as well; and discusses not just wars and battles but military writings such as Sun Tzu and Clausewitz as well as some broad historical processes that have impinged on military history, pushing it along and being pushed by it.

As Woodrow Wilson, himself a historian (though not a military one), once said, addressing a big subject at length is fairly easy. Doing the same briefly can be very difficult. In fact, it was precisely the difficulty of the task that appealed to me and made me take up the challenge. But how to go about it? Where to start? Where to end? How to arrange the material? What to put in and what, more importantly, to leave out? The following pages are, among other things, an attempt to answer these questions.

Martin van Creveld
Jerusalem
2017

THE
ASCENT OF WAR

10,000 BCE–476 CE

1

The Beginning of War?

c. 10,000 BCE

Archaeological finds from Jebel Shaba, in the Sudan, and Nataruk, in Kenya, indicate that groups of nomadic, hunting-gathering members of the species *Homo sapiens sapiens* had begun waging war on each other.

Evidence for deadly human-on-human violence goes back at least as far as 50,000 BCE. It consists of weapons, such as stone-made spear and arrow points; bones that have been broken, crushed or perforated; and, occasionally, graves. However, such violence on its own does not amount to war. Whether early humans understood the differences between crime, police action, feuding, war, and genocide in ways similar to our present understanding of these things is doubtful. Thinking of it, it seems rather unlikely. What Jebel Shaba and Nataruk do prove, though, is that 12,000 or so years ago humans were engaging in *collective* violence against each other.

The motives that drove our remote ancestors to engage in war must have resembled those found in more recent, and much better known, hunting-gathering societies. They probably included conflicts over access to natural resources such as watering places and hunting grounds; disputes over women and the sexual and reproductive possibilities they offered; the need to avenge insults of every kind; and general competition.

Normally the warring societies must have lived fairly close together, though there may have been exceptions to that

What the earliest warriors probably looked like.

rule. Tactically, conflicts probably took the form of skirmishes, ambushes, and raids. The time and location of some encounters may have been prearranged. Each 'campaign' separately was short, lasting no more than hours or, at most, days. However, the frequent recurrence of hostilities meant that, relative to the size of the warring societies, over time casualties could amount to a considerable part of the populations involved. The findings at Nataruk seem to show that no one was spared. In later tribal warfare, though, while adult men would be slaughtered, young women and children were more often taken prisoner. Either way, entire societies could be, and presumably sometimes were, wiped out.

Recent discoveries in the field put an end to the common, but mistaken, idea that war only emerged after the agricultural revolution led to a surplus and made settled communities possible. In other words, *le bon sauvage* is a myth. This does not, however, necessarily mean that our ancestors were incapable of friendship, altruism, kindness, or love.

2 Beginning of the Bronze Age

c. 3500 BCE

The earliest raw materials from which weapons were made were bone (for spear and arrow points), stone (used, in addition to points, for maces and knives), wood (for shafts, clubs, and bows and arrows; bows are a very ancient weapon, going back to at least 60,000 BCE); and linen, hemp, silk, sinews, and rawhide (for bowstrings). The middle of the fourth millennium BCE saw the introduction of bronze in the Indus Valley. From there it spread north-eastward to China and Korea, as well as westward into the Middle East and Europe.

As this list implies, the ingredients of bronze – copper and tin – may be found in many different places around the world. Harder than copper, whose military use was essentially limited to maces, it could be moulded into any desirable shape and sharpened to a fine edge (though some earlier weapons, made of obsidian or animal teeth, could be very sharp indeed). It also lasted longer than organic materials did. These advantages

The first weapons were made of stone, wood and bone.

explain why it was used to manufacture, among other things, weapons such as spear and arrow points, swords, daggers, axes, and halberds. Later defensive equipment such as helmets, shields, armour, and greaves were added.

Manufacturing bronze requires quite sophisticated technology. Such technology in turn presupposes specialised craftsmen as well as permanent settlements. Societies that did not form such settlements could not produce it, though they may have acquired the weapons by trade or plunder. In the most advanced societies bronze remained the main material for manufacture of military equipment until about 1000 BCE, when it started to be replaced by iron and steel.

3

The Battle of Banquan

c. 2650 BCE

Described in Sima Qian's *Records of the Grand Historian* (*c.* 100 BCE), the Battle of Banquan is often considered the earliest recorded battle in history. However, over two millennia passed from the time the battle took place to its being mentioned in the *Records*. As a result, the details are somewhat obscure. Not only is the exact location where it took place disputed, but it may actually have consisted of three separate battles which subsequent generations, less interested in the military detail, compressed into one.

The antagonists were Yandi, 'The Flame Emperor', on one side and Huangdi, or 'Yellow Emperor', on the other. During most of China's history Huangdi was regarded as a key figure in the creation of Chinese civilisation. However, not long after the overthrow of imperial rule in 1911 CE he lost that status and came to be considered a legendary or, at best, semi-legendary figure. Among the many useful devices Huangdi is supposed

Did ancient Chinese commanders look like this?

to have invented was the first bow. Climbing a mulberry tree to escape a tiger, he used a stone knife to fashion it out of the surrounding branches as well as the vine that was growing on it. His men, belonging to the Youxiong tribe, prevailed over their enemies, the Shennong. The latter seem to have been nomads who entered the North China Plain from the north and the east, starting a pattern that was to shape Chinese history for the next 4,000 years or so.

After the battle, Yandi was murdered, leading to the amalgamation of the two tribes. Together they formed the Huaxia ('grand beautiful') people, generally seen as the ancestor of China's Han civilisation.

The Battle of Kadesh

1274 BCE

This clash between Pharaoh Ramses II of Egypt and the Hittite King Muwatalli II is the earliest of which we have a detailed account, complete with information about formations, weapons and tactics. Most of the information is contained in reliefs and inscriptions Ramses had made and put up in various temples. Hittite records also mention the battle, though in far less detail.

In the spring Ramses and his army, consisting of about 20,000 men, divided into four brigades with about 2,000 chariots between them, left Egypt. Marching by way of the Sinai and Canaan (Palestine), he entered Syria from the south-west. There he almost fell into a trap as some local people, perhaps Hittite spies, informed him the enemy was still 200km away. In fact, the distance between the two forces was only about 11km. As a result, when the Hittites attacked Ramses only had two of his four brigades immediately available. Said to be 'more numerous than the grains of sand on the beach',[*] the enemy easily broke through the Egyptian array.

If Ramses' account may be believed, at one point he was left on his own, with 'no officer, no charioteer, no soldier of the army, no shield-bearer'[†] to help him. What saved him was the god

---

[*] Quoted in J. Tyldesley, *Ramesses II: Egypt's Greatest Pharaoh* (London: Penguin Books, 2000), pp. 70–1.

[†] Quoted in M. Lichtheim, *Ancient Egyptian Literature. II: The New Kingdom* (Berkeley: University of California Press, 1976), p. 65.

Amun, hard fighting, and, above all, the fact that the Hittites smelled victory. Abandoning the pursuit, the Hittites turned and started plundering the Egyptian camp – probably not the first, and certainly not the last, time such a thing happened. The remaining Egyptian brigades arrived on the field and counter-attacked. They drove the enemy into the nearby river Orontes, killing many and forcing others to swim across 'like crocodiles'[‡] so as to make their escape.

The relatively plentiful information we have about it apart, the battle is remarkable for the fact that it was fought with the aid of as many as 5,000 horse-drawn chariots on both sides. This makes it the largest such encounter in history. Apparently the Egyptian chariots proved lighter, faster and more manoeuvrable than the Hittite ones.

The day ended with what may have been a tactical victory for the Egyptians. However, they were unable to maintain themselves in Syria. Over the next fifteen years the two sides continued to fight each other in northern Palestine and south-ern Syria. Hostilities were finally concluded in 1258 BCE by means of a treaty, a copy of which is now in the Istanbul Archaeological Museum.

[‡] Quoted in R. Overy, *A History of War in 100 Battles* (London: HarperCollins, 2014), p. 323.

5

Beginning of the
Trojan War*

The reasons that led to the Trojan War – the kidnap or elopement of Helen by or with Paris of Troy, the jilted Menelaus' ability to persuade his brother Agamemnon, King of Mycenae, to retrieve her, and the subsequent campaign – do not need repeating in detail. Suffice it to say that it lasted for ten years before the city finally fell. The *Iliad*, on which all other literary sources drew, gives the number of Greeks as 50,000 and that of Trojans as 10,000. By another interpretation the figures were 250,000 and 50,000 respectively. No fewer than a thousand ships carried the Greeks to their destination. Without question, the poem vastly exaggerates both the length of the war and the number of participants. Almost certainly what we are talking about is a raid that lasted days or weeks, involving no more than a few hundred men on each side.

The organisation, weapons, and tactics on both sides have given rise to more controversy than can be dealt with here. Perhaps the most interesting feature, seldom mentioned, is the fact that at no point in the story is there any mention of siege techniques: No ramps, no mantelets warriors can use as shelter,

---

* According to the calculations of the third-century BCE Alexandrian polymath Eratosthenes.

Homer was blind, yet understood war as well as anyone before or since.

and no battering rams. No ladders even. The fighting consisted almost entirely of face-to-face duels between aristocratic heroes who often knew each other by name. It took place exclusively in the open. That is why, in the end, the Greeks had to resort to a *ruse de guerre*, the famous Trojan horse, in order to get inside the walls and capture the city. Yet in Mesopotamia all the above-mentioned siege devices had been in use since at least 1600 BCE.

What gives this particular raid its extraordinary importance is the great early seventh-century BCE poem that was built around it. Never in the whole of history has anyone excelled Homer – who according to tradition was blind – in describing the joy of war, its glory, its sorrows, and its horrors: the place it occupies in human life. Clearly to command and fight in war are one thing, to put the experience into words, let alone words that will echo through millennia, quite another.

6

First Naval Battle on Record

1186 BCE

The first naval battle on record was fought in one of the mouths of the Nile, where it flows into the Mediterranean. The details are known from inscriptions and reliefs set up by the Egyptian Pharaoh Ramses III. The enemy were the so-called Sea People, apparently a loose alliance of tribes originating in Cyprus, Crete, and perhaps even as far away as Sardinia. By this time they had been raiding the eastern Mediterranean, including not just Egypt but the coasts of Phoenicia and Palestine, for a century past. Some probably used that region as a base from which to attack Egypt.

Having received intelligence about the approaching invasion, Ramses hurried north 'like a whirlwind'. Next, he says, 'a net was prepared to ensnare [the enemy]':

> I caused the Nile mouths to be prepared like a strong wall with warships, galleys and coasters, equipped, for they were manned completely from bow to stem with valiant warriors with their weapons ... As for those who came forward together on the sea, the full flame [presumably the Egyptian fleet] was in front of them at the Nile mouths, while a stockade of lances surrounded them on the shore [so that they were] dragged [ashore], hemmed in, prostrated on the beach, slain, made into heaps from head to tail. Their ships and their goods were as if fallen into the water.[*]

Warships go back over 3,000 years.

Vivid images, originally painted in bright colours, accompany the text.

They show five enemy ships, distinguished by birds' heads at both ends, and four Egyptian ones, identifiable by the lioness heads on their prows. The Egyptian ships all point in the same direction; not so the enemy ones. Perhaps this was meant to indicate that the latter were taken by surprise. Weapons included bows, arrows, spears, and swords. Meanwhile grappling hooks prevented the enemy vessels from escaping. We also see Egyptian soldiers dragging their enemies out of the water and binding them.

The outcome was a victory for Ramses and the end of the Sea People's threat to Egypt. But they did not disappear. Exploiting the collapse of the Hittite Empire a few years earlier, they were able to establish permanent settlements along the south Palestinian coast.

* Quoted in E. Velikovsky, *Ages in Chaos, Vol. III: Peoples of the Sea* (Garden City, NJ: Doubleday, 1977), p. 69.

7

Incipient Shift from Bronze to Iron Weapons

c. 1000 BCE

The transition from bronze to iron seems to have started in Central Asia. From there it passed to China and Europe, where it was well under way in 750 BCE. Iron ore was much easier to find, though more difficult to work, than deposits of tin. Iron itself had the advantage that it was much harder than bronze and not nearly as brittle. First it was sharpened to create edged weapons. Later technical improvements also enabled it to be hammered into shape to produce defensive equipment of every kind.

The most efficient army of the period was the Assyrian one. It is known to us from numerous inscriptions (in cuneiform), administrative documents written on clay, reliefs, and the Old Testament. The latter provides the following chilling description of it:

> And he [the Lord] will lift up an ensign to the nations from far, and will hiss unto them from the end of the earth; and behold, they shall come with speed swiftly; none shall be weary nor stumble among them; none shall slumber nor sleep; neither shall the girdle of their loins be loosed, nor the latchet of their shoes be broken; whose arrows are sharp, and all their bows bent, their horses' hoofs shall be counted like flint, and their wheels like a whirlwind; their roaring shall be like a lion, they shall roar like young lions; yes they shall roar, and lay hold of the prey and shall carry it safe, and none shall deliver it.

An Assyrian soldier, recognisable by his peculiar pointed helmet.

At peak, shortly before 700 BCE, the army was a full-time, integrated fighting force capable of year-round operations. It consisted of spear-carrying infantry, archers, slingers, cavalry, and chariots. The Assyrian troops proper, easily recognisable by their pointed helmets, were often accompanied by auxiliaries as well as men raised in the conquered provinces. We know of captains of ten and captains of fifty. Some were eunuchs, others not. The officers' symbol of authority was the mace, though apparently not all carried it.

Perhaps the most impressive aspect of the army was its highly developed siege technique, complete with ladders, ramps, rams, mantelets, and mining. To this was added a reputation for extreme cruelty generated by the use and celebration of punishments such as decapitation, flaying, and impalement. Emperor Tiglath-Pileser III, on a monument he set up in 734 BCE, boasted that his conquests extended 'from the horizon to heaven'.[*] It was an exaggeration, but not a very great one.

---

[*]   Quoted in Encyclopedia.com, at www.encyclopedia.com/history/ encyclopedias-almanacs-transcripts-and-maps/tiglath-pileser-iii

8 Birth Year of Sun Tzu

Assuming he was a historical figure, which some dispute, Sun Tzu was a commander and a scholar. He is remembered as the author of *The Art of War*, probably the greatest military treatise ever written.

The most important fact about *The Art of War*, often overlooked by Western students, is that it is a Daoist text in the tradition of Lao Tzu ('Old Teacher'). In this context, *Dao*, usually translated as 'The Way', means achieving such perfection that things will move of themselves, so to speak.

Basically war is a departure from The Way. Nevertheless, given that it comprises 'the road to survival or ruin', it must be thoroughly studied. The prospect of success must be estimated in terms of:

1. The strength of the bonds that, on both sides, link ruler and troops
2. The weather
3. The terrain
4. The qualities of the commander
5. Military organisation, command and control, and logistics

War is waged against a living, thinking opponent as intelligent as oneself. To succeed in it, one must employ a combination of force and stratagem, all the while avoiding prolonged conflict,

Sun Tzu (541–494 BCE) may well have been the greatest military theoretician of all time.

from which no state, ruler, or people have ever benefited. The best way to achieve this is by diplomacy. If a commander is too obtuse to use that, then he should resort to dirty tricks. If not dirty tricks, then manoeuvre; if not manoeuvre, then battle; and if not battle, then siege. All of this while taking into consideration factors such as geography, the season of the year, and 'moral force', meaning the extent to which each side maintains its own customs, laws, and regulations.

Use the maximum amount of brains, the minimum amount of force. To do so, rely on your knowledge of the enemy (i.e. intelligence) in order to deceive him. If you are strong, pretend to be weak. If you are weak, pretend to be strong. If you are at X, pretend to be at Y. If you are at Y, pretend to be at X. Confuse the enemy and unbalance him. Then, at the decisive moment, surprise him by falling upon him and smashing him as a rock smashes an egg.

Tradition has it that Sun Tzu died in 494 BCE. Since then, not only has *The Art of War* been reissued in countless editions and translations, but today on Google the author has 1,800,000 hits – more than enough to justify his inclusion here.

9 First Persian Invasion of Greece

490 BCE

This is also the first war for which we have a complete, well-researched book relying on eyewitnesses, namely Herodotus' *History*.

Persia at the time was the greatest power in the world, reaching from the frontier of India to the Hellespont. The background to the war was formed by Athens' assistance to the Ionian revolt, mounted by the Greeks of western Asia Minor, against Persian rule. Earlier, in 492 BCE, the Persians had subdued Macedonia and Thrace. They were, however, unable to hold on and forced to withdraw.

In 490 they came again, this time by sea. Landing at Marathon, nor far from Athens, with perhaps as many as 25,000 infantry and 1,000 cavalry. The Athenian army may have numbered 10,000 heavy infantrymen (hoplites). Forming a phalanx, they stormed forward. As they did so the wings got ahead of the centre – whether on purpose or accidentally is not clear. Caught in between the two wings, the lightly armoured Persians panicked and fled to their ships. Thousands died, at relatively small cost to the Greeks.

Eight years later the Persians returned. This time they brought a huge army with 900,000 men and 4,327 ships. A Greek (Spartan) attempt to stop the invasion at Thermopylae failed as the Persians found a road around the pass. Thereupon the

A Greek hoplite.

Athenians, on the advice of their leader Themistocles, decided to abandon their city. While the Persians burnt Athens, the two fleets met in the Bay of Salamis. In the narrow waters of the bay the Greek fleet, made up of smaller, more agile vessels, was at an advantage and won a great victory, after which King Xerxes left the country, leaving in command Mardonius.

The penultimate act of the great drama took place at Platea, in Boeotia, in the spring of 479. Here some 80,000 Greek hoplites confronted what was probably a similar number of Persian troops. As at Marathon, the lightly armed Persians could not resist the onslaught of the phalanx coming at them. Many were caught in their camp where Mardonius himself was killed. Fought on the same day as a second naval action, this time at Mycale near the south-eastern coast of Anatolia, the battle effectively ended the invasion.

The two wars together saved Greece from ever becoming part of the Persian Empire. A century and a half later they provided Alexander the Great with an excuse to start his own conquest of Persia.

10

Outbreak of the Peloponnesian War

The Peloponnesian War was the largest fought in Europe to date. As the historian Thucydides says, 'the real cause' (*aitia*) of the war was Sparta's fear of Athens' power, which had been steadily growing ever since the Persian Wars of 490–80 BCE. Sparta was primarily a land power, Athens a naval one. Aware of the strength of the Spartan army with its massed infantry fighting in a phalanx, the Athenians did not dare meet them on land. Instead they withdrew behind their fortifications, leaving the enemy free to ravage the surrounding countryside. At the same time they sent naval expeditions to the Peloponnese in the hope of detaching Sparta's allies, making the enslaved Helots revolt, and causing trouble in general.

Neither strategy worked very well. The Spartans found the Athenians safe behind their walls. Reaching all the way to the port of Piraeus, they enabled the city to continue trading and importing food almost undisturbed, although the overcrowding caused by refugees from the countryside did cause a plague that killed thousands of people, the great leader Pericles included. The Athenians' attempts to destabilise the Lacedaemonian alliance did not fare much better. In 421 BCE the two sides agreed on the so-called Peace of Nicias, which restored the *status quo ante*, more or less.

In 415 BCE, using as an excuse the fact that the largest city on Sicily, Syracuse, was attacking one of their allies, the Athenians

Greek hoplites in a phalanx, in the standby position.

decided to invade the island in an attempt to conquer it. As Syracuse defended itself, the Athenian expedition was trapped in the city's harbour and annihilated. Meanwhile the Spartans, acting on the advice of an Athenian renegade, Alcibiades, set up a permanent garrison at Decelea, near Athens. The slaves working the silver mines on which Athens depended for its wealth were freed and the mines brought to a standstill, delivering a heavy blow to the city's economy.

Still the war went on, with Alcibiades, now back in Athens, providing leadership. The turning point came when Sparta, receiving financial assistance from Athens' great enemy Persia, built a navy. During the first couple of naval battles fought between the two sides, the Athenians had little difficulty overpowering the less experienced Spartans. However, in 405 BCE the Spartan commander Lysander all but annihilated the Athenian fleet at Aegospotami, not far from the Hellespont, through which Athens' vital imports of grain passed. Faced with starvation, Athens surrendered.

11

The Invention of Mechanical Artillery

<u>399 BCE</u>

By 399 BCE, practically all the elements of pre-gunpowder fortification – ditches, crenelated curtain walls, glacis, machicolation, fortified gates, and portcullises – had long been in existence. About the only missing element was the round tower, which started replacing square ones shortly after 1100 CE.

It was to overcome these defences that the ruler of Syracuse, Dionysius I, had his engineers develop the first mechanical artillery devices. The raw material was wood, with iron nails and dowels to hold the parts together. The engines fell into two basic types: stone-throwers and arrow-firers.

Stone-throwers (ballistae) were powered by skeins of twisted cords. They threw stones on an indirect (high) trajectory. The largest models could launch a stone weighing a talent (anything between 20kg and 50kg) to a distance of 200–300m. Normally such machines were not sufficiently powerful to demolish walls, but by throwing their loads over them they could certainly kill and injure the people inside as well as demolishing houses.

Arrow-firers (catapults) were essentially outsized crossbows. Mounted on tripods, they fired their iron bolts in in a direct (straight) trajectory. The largest ones were powered by twisted cords; the smaller ones, by springs. Such engines were useful for clearing sections of the walls of their defenders, thus enabling other troops to approach the walls, build ramps, put battering

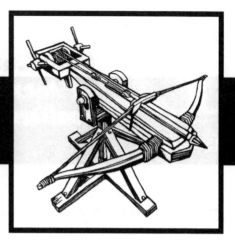

The invention of catapults in 399 BCE revolutionised siege warfare.

rams in place, etc. The Romans used similar but smaller engines in field warfare too. During the first century BCE each legion probably had a few dozen of them.

Another fourth-century BCE innovation was the siege tower. Towers, some of them 40m high, were made of wood. They were covered with wet leather to protect them against fire and provided with rollers that enabled them to be moved close to the walls, hence the medieval nickname for them, *malvoisins*, or 'bad neighbours'. Archers, positioned on top, fired at the defenders. Next, a bridge would be lowered so as to enable them to seize the walls and engage in hand-to-hand combat.

Working closely with rams and mechanical artillery, towers revolutionised siegecraft. The latter reached its apogee around 300 BCE in the hands of Demetrius Poliorcetes (Demetrius the City-Taker). From then until the end of the middle ages the only important technical development in the field was the trebuchet, a counterweight-operated machine first developed in China which reached Europe around 1200 CE.

12

First Campaign of Alexander* the Great

338 BCE

Commanding the Macedonian cavalry at Chaeronea in 338 BCE, Alexander helped his father Philip II inflict a heavy defeat on the opposing Greek forces. Two years later, following Philip's assassination, he succeeded to the throne.

In 334 BCE Alexander, at the head of a mixed force consisting of Macedonians and Greeks, set out to conquer the Persian Empire, the greatest power of the age. First he defeated the Persians on the river Granicus, thus opening the way into Asia Minor. Next came the larger Battle of Issus, which led to the conquest of Syria. Turning south, Alexander besieged and captured the cities of Tyre and Gaza. From there he continued along the coasts of Palestine and the Sinai, reaching Egypt, which fell without battle.

In 331 BCE Alexander, with an estimated 47,000 men, met a Persian army perhaps twice as large at Gaugamela (Arbela), near the present-day Kurdish city of Erbil. His cavalry and infantry inflicted a crushing defeat on the emperor, Darius III, who fled but was killed soon after. From there Alexander marched on Babylon in Mesopotamia, which was then one of the world's largest cities, and then on to the Persian capital of

* The name means 'Defender of Men'.

Alexander ('the Great') of Macedon.

Persepolis, which he sacked and burnt. He spent the next five years campaigning in present-day Iran and Afghanistan, fighting countless small battles and capturing many strongholds.

The year 326 BCE found Alexander on the borders of India where he defeated King Porus and invaded his country. What drove him was an insatiable desire for power and fame; as he said, had it depended on him he would have continued his march and conquered not only India but 'the ends of the world and the great outer sea'.[†] In the event his troops mutinied, forcing him to turn back to Babylon. There, aged 32, he died in 323 BCE.

Starting in antiquity, opinions about Alexander have always been divided. Some hailed him as an enlightened ruler bent on creating a new cosmopolitan order. Others saw him as a ruthless monster who did not know when to stop. Seemingly the only thing about him not in dispute is that he was a military prodigy the likes of whom the world has seldom, if ever, seen.

[†] Arrian, *Anabasis*, 5.24.8.

13

Outbreak of the Punic Wars

Accoording to tradition, Rome was founded in 751 BCE. From then on it constantly fought other Italian cities and tribes from whom, says the historian Livy, its people differed in 'nothing except courage'.[*] In 280–79 BCE Rome's armies repulsed King Pyrrhus of Epirus, one of the greatest commanders of the age, who had invaded south-eastern Italy. This victory made it the undisputed mistress of the peninsula.

In 264 BCE the Romans invaded Sicily, which previously had been allied with Carthage. The ensuing twenty-three-year-long struggle unfolded partly on the island, partly in the surrounding seas, and partly in Africa. First the Romans forced the largest city in Sicily, Syracuse, to renounce its Carthaginian alliance and join them. Then they built a fleet almost from scratch and equipped it with a new device, the *corvus* (raven). It consisted of a heavy iron hook attached to a bridge that could be lowered from a ship's mast, linking it to the enemy vessel and enabling the Romans to fight as if on land. A Roman landing in Africa was repulsed. However, in the end what counted was the naval war. In 241 BCE, following its defeat in the Battle of the Aegates Islands, Carthage was forced to give up Sicily and pay a heavy indemnity.

In 218 BCE the war resumed. Using Spain, now a Carthaginian colony, as his base, Hannibal crossed the Alps and invaded Italy. Between 218 and 216 he inflicted three crushing defeats

[*] Livy, *The History of Rome*, 8.8.

The *corvus* ('raven') enabled Roman troops to fight at sea as if on land.

on the Romans: at Trebia, at Lake Trasimene, and at Cannae. Apparently not feeling strong enough, though, he refrained from marching on Rome. Instead he spent the years 216–14 in southern Italy, ravaging it, defeating the forces sent against him, and trying, without much success, to detach Rome's allies. In 214 the Romans launched a seaborne expedition against Syracuse, which had joined Carthage, and captured it. In 207 a second Carthaginian army, sent from Spain to assist Hannibal, was defeated at the Metaurus, leaving him isolated.

Meanwhile the Romans were trying to take Spain away from Carthage. Their first attempts, made in 212–10, were defeated. However, the arrival of a new Roman commander, Scipio, changed the situation. In 206 the Battle of Ilipa left the whole of Spain in Roman hands.

In 203 the Carthaginian Senate recalled Hannibal from Italy. A year later the two sides met at Zama. Scipio crushed Hannibal, who was forced to flee. In the peace treaty the Romans stripped Carthage of most of its remaining territory, extracted a huge indemnity, and disarmed it. The war left Rome mistress of the western and central Mediterranean.

14

Construction of China's Great Wall Begins

220 BCE

Following China's unification at the hands of Emperor Qin Shi Huang (221 BCE), the only remaining serious military threat facing the country was the one presented by the so-called 'northern barbarians'. To contain these nomadic tribes, construction began on a wall, building on earlier foundations. Over time the job developed into a gigantic enterprise that was to occupy various Chinese rulers for over a millennium and a half to come.

As the length of the period in question implies, the wall was built not all at once but piecemeal, section by section, by different rulers. In the process, old sections were often abandoned, allowed to decay, and later rebuilt and incorporated into more recent defensive works. At its peak, under the Ming Dynasty (1368–1644 CE), the wall was some 5,000km long, 5–7m

Built over a period of centuries, the Great Wall of China remains the largest construction project in history.

tall, and 5m wide on top. Forming part of an elaborate defensive system, it was reinforced by as many as 25,000 watchtowers and, at places, various kinds of earthworks.

Enormous as it was, the wall never offered complete protection against the barbarians. Twice, in 1271 and again in 1644–62, it failed to prevent some of those barbarians from overrunning China, ousting its rulers, and founding new dynasties. Built by conscripted peasants at the cost of as many as a million lives, today the wall remains the largest construction project, military or civilian, of all time.

15

Opening of Rome's Conquest of the Eastern Mediterranean

In the background in this period was the alliance of King Philip V of Macedon with Hannibal (215 BCE). Making use of the fact that Rome's hands were tied, Philip expanded his rule in Illyria as well Greece and the Aegean. Two years after Zama, Rome took its revenge.

At Cynoscephalae in 196 BCE the Romans crushed the Macedonians. Six years later they and their allies defeated King Antiochus III of Syria, first at Thermopylae, then in the naval battle of Eurymedon, and finally at Magnesia in Asia Minor.

In 170 BCE the Romans went to war again. This time their victim was Philip's son, Perseus. Having defeated him, they dismantled his kingdom. Twenty-four years later, in 146 BCE, they simultaneously crushed both their old enemy, Carthage, and the Achaean League, as the only independent power left in Greece. In both cases the principal enemy cities, Carthage and Corinth, were utterly destroyed, though both were later rebuilt.

Looking back to the Punic Wars, militarily speaking two main factors made this unprecedented string of successes possible. First, thanks to the system of treaties they had built in Italy, the Romans had at their disposal a pool of manpower far larger than

Roman legionaries. Livy says they were no better than anyone else, except in courage.

that of any contemporary country or ruler. Second, they had developed a military formation – the legion – which was probably superior to any other until the late eighteenth century CE.

As described by the second-century BCE Greek historian Polybius, the legion numbered 4,200 of whom 200 were spear-carrying cavalrymen. The rest consisted of heavy (armoured) infantry armed with javelins and swords. Also part of the legion was a company of engineers to operate the artillery, plan fortified camps, etc. The basic fighting unit was the maniple, some 160 men strong and made up of two centuries. Later the maniples were grouped into ten cohorts. In battle the maniples, arrayed in three lines, formed the famous chequerboard formation. Command and control was assured by means of auditory and visual signals (standards). The outcome was an unprecedented combination of resilience and flexibility infinitely superior to the powerful but unwieldy Graeco-Macedonian phalanx.

16

Outbreak of the Roman Civil Wars

Politically, the Roman Republic's greatest strength had always been the fact that, for a period of some four centuries, its domestic life was peaceful. However, in 91 BCE the Italian allies demanded full citizenship. Scarcely had the ensuing war ended, and the Italians achieved their demands, than the two principal Roman commanders of the age, Marius and Sulla, representing the *populares* (people) and the *optimates* (nobles) respectively, fell out with each other. Mainly conducted in and around Rome, this struggle was extremely bloody before it finally ended in Sulla's complete victory.

In Marius' hands, the Roman army became a full-time professional force comprising many property-less men with nothing to lose. Such armies followed their commanders who could and did use them as they saw fit, including waging war on other Roman commanders and the Senate itself.

The next most important figure was Pompey (nicknamed 'the Great'). In 82–79 BCE he campaigned against pirates in Sicily, the followers of Marius in Africa, rebellious tribesmen in Spain, and the slave commander Spartacus in Italy itself. Next, in 66–62, he subdued Armenia and, not even bothering to inform the Senate, conquered Syria and Palestine.

Returning to Rome, in 61 BCE Pompey formed an alliance (*triumvirate*) with two other commanders, Julius Caesar and Marcus Crassus. Crassus set out to wage war on Parthia, in the course of which campaign his army was destroyed and he himself

Julius Caesar, affectionately known to his soldiers as 'the bald fornicator'.

killed. Meanwhile Caesar spent ten years (59–49 BCE) fighting in Gaul before the country was finally subdued. Returning to Rome with his army in 49 BCE, he was appointed *dictator*. First he went to Spain where he defeated Pompey's supporters. Next he pursued Pompey and defeated him at the Battle of Pharsalus (48 BCE).

Caesar spent the next years annexing Egypt and Pontus (47 BCE) and fighting Pompey's last supporters in Africa and Spain. Returning to Rome, in 44 BCE he was assassinated. His death started a new round of civil wars. The first was fought between Caesar's assassins and his self-appointed heirs, Octavian and Marcus Antonius; this round ended at the Battle of Philippi, in Thrace, in 42 BCE. Next, Octavian and Antonius fell out. Hostilities started in 33 BCE and ended two years later in Octavian's victory in the naval battle of Actium, whereupon the Republic came to an end and the Principate was firmly established.

These years saw Roman warfare at its bloody zenith. In particular, Caesar ('I came, I saw, I conquered') must be counted among the greatest warlords of all time.

17

The Battle of the Teutoburg Forest

The battle of the Teutoburg Forest was fought between the Roman commander Varus and a coalition of German tribes under Hermann the Cheruscan. On the Roman side it represented an attempt, starting fifteen years earlier but interrupted by a massive rebellion in the Balkans, to subdue large parts of Germany east of the Rhine.

Hermann (Arminius) had been educated in Rome and served in the Roman army. In the autumn of 9 CE Varus, with three legions and some auxiliary units, was on his way back from the Weser, where he had been campaigning, to winter quarters on the Rhine. With him was Hermann, who had suggested the route. In the forest, located north of modern Osnabrück, Hermann defected to the other side. Next he and his men ambushed the Romans. Caught strung out in marching order, the latter were annihilated.

Octavian, now known as the Emperor Augustus, deeply resented the defeat. In his political testament he told his successors to refrain from trying to expand the borders of the empire. This did not prevent the first of those successors, Tiberius, from sending his nephew, Germanicus, on a series of huge campaigns in Germany aimed at avenging Varus and re-establishing Roman deterrence. However, no further attempt was made to establish a permanent presence in the lands in question. To that extent, Augustus' will was adhered to.

Taking a wider perspective, the Roman army had always consisted primarily of heavy infantry intended to defeat its enemies in battle and engage in sieges. It was less effective in countries where there were no open fields to deploy, no enemies who fought pitched battles, and no cities to capture, but which offered plenty of space for the enemy to retreat. Thus the Battle of the Teutoburg Forest, like that of Carrhae in 53 BCE where Crassus had been defeated, marked the limits of what Roman military power could do.

18

The Battle of Adrianople

378 CE

From at least the time of Augustus on, Rome had been the undisputed mistress of the *oikumene*, or 'known world'. Though countless wars took place on the frontiers and, especially after 235 CE, inside the empire between different claimants to the throne, none really challenged this supremacy. However, around the 370s CE things started changing as the pressure from barbarian tribes, coming from the north, grew.

In 376 CE the Goths under Fritigern, pressed by other tribes, asked for permission from the eastern emperor, Valens, to cross the Danube and settle. Permission was granted, but once the Goths were inside they felt mistreated by local Roman officials and started ravaging throughout the Balkans. Valens called on the western emperor, his nephew Gratian, for military assistance and received it. In the end, though, Valens decided to give battle before Gratian's forces could join him.

By this time the Roman army had undergone great changes. Ethnically it was made up of men of every nation and tribe under the sun. Among them were many barbarians from outside the borders, some of whom served in their own units under their own chiefs. The legions had become smaller, whereas the role of cavalry and light troops, such as archers and slingers, had grown. In terms of numbers, the forces were fairly evenly matched, with about 15–30,000 men on each side.

The details are known from Ammianus Marcellinus, a Roman officer and an eyewitness. Having marched for seven hours over difficult terrain, the Roman troops arrived tired and dehydrated. They attacked the Gothic circle of wagons; however, the Goths having set the surrounding fields on fire, they were obstructed by heat and smoke. A further delay was occasioned by negotiations, giving Fritigern time to recall his cavalry, which had been foraging. Returning to the field, the cavalry took the Romans at the rear. Assisted by Fritigern's infantry, which seized the opportunity to burst out of the wagon circle and counter-attack, the cavalry pressed the Romans against a nearby hill, where they were unable to manoeuvre, and routed them. Even though about a third of the troops got away, Valens himself was killed. Thereafter peace was restored, but only at the cost of leaving the Goths in possession of much of the Balkans.

There had been many previous battles between Rome and the barbarians, most of which the Romans won. Taken on its own, the one at Adrianople was too small to determine the fate of the empire. It did, however, mark an important stage in the process by which the advantage gradually passed to the barbarians until Rome itself was sacked in 410 CE.

19 Publication of Vegetius' *Epitoma Rei Militaris*

c. 400 CE

Who Vegetius was we do not know. He may have been an officer whose work was commissioned by one of two emperors named Theodosius, but this has been disputed. The purpose of his book, *Epitoma rei militaris*, was to point to the decadence of the Roman army, which after Adrianople must have become obvious, and suggest ways to reform it.

While constantly mentioning 'the ancients', the *Epitoma* does not describe the army as it was at any particular time. Instead it is a compilation – albeit a remarkably coherent one – made up of various sources dating from various periods. The text mentions books by Cato the Elder (second century BCE), Sallust, Cornelius Celsus (both first century BCE), Frontinus (*c.* 100 CE), as well as works by the emperors Augustus, Trajan, and Hadrian.

Part 1 discusses recruitment, training, and the formations to be used in battle. Part 2 gives the best account of the legion we have or are likely to have. That includes its organisation; the sub-units of which it consisted; the officers; the promotion system; the auxiliary services; the troop of horse; and the way in which it ought to be drawn up for battle. Part 3 deals with the

various tactical methods the legion used. This part ends with a long list of dos and don'ts. Part 4, which seems to have been tagged on by another writer, discusses fortifications and naval warfare. From beginning to end, the importance of thorough training, strong discipline, hard work, and sound planning are emphasised.

The book is succinct and well written. Dedicated to an emperor, it had a direct link with the prestige of imperial Rome; it also contains many useful suggestions in regard to fortification in particular. These facts explain why, for over a thousand years after it was published, it easily remained the most popular Western military handbook of all. As late as 1770, one Austrian field marshal, the Prince de Ligne, went so far as to claim that 'Vegetius had been inspired by God'.[*]

---

[*] J. Clarke (trans.), 'The Military Institutions of the Romans' (2001), at www.digitalattic.org/home/war/vegetius, introduction.

20

Battle of the Catalaunian Plains

451 CE

Approaching from the east, Attila and his Huns crossed the Rhine, sacking cities on their way and advancing as far as Aurelianum (the modern Orléans). Laying siege to it, they found it strongly defended. This enabled Flavius Aetius, the Roman *magister militum* (best translated as commander-in-chief), to come to the rescue. However, his forces were insufficient to take on the Huns on their own. Accordingly he convinced a number of rulers of Germanic tribes, the most important of whom was Theodoric I, King of the Visigoths, to join him. Meeting at Toulouse, together the allies marched on Orléans to relieve it.

By one source, diviners told Attila – he who said that where he passed no grass would ever grow again –that an enemy commander would be killed but that the Huns would be defeated. Thereupon Attila suspended the siege and marched east with Aetius in pursuit. The two armies, each probably 50–80,000 men strong, met at the Catalaunian Plains, near today's Châlons. The field was dominated by a ridge, which became the epicentre of the struggle as both sides tried to occupy it. The decisive move was made by the Visigoths.

Attila the Hun may have looked like this – or perhaps not.

Apparently occupying the allied centre, they attacked and forced the Huns back into their camp, consisting of a wagon circle. The number of casualties was high on both sides, but the Hunnic one in particular was said to be immense.

In the process, Theodoric was killed and had to be disinterred from under the mountain of corpses that covered him. Next morning, Aetius, reluctant to share the glory with his allies, was able to convince them to go home. Instead of pushing the siege of Attila's camp to its logical end, he allowed him and his Huns to depart. Possibly he was already thinking of him as a future ally against the Visigoths. Thus the battle, though it did remove the Huns' threat to Gaul, did not mark their final defeat. It was, however, the last hurrah of the western Roman Empire, which came to an end twenty-five years later.

Part II

MEDIEVAL WAR

476-1494 CE

21

Opening of Justinian's Campaigns

533

Justinian's campaigns aimed at rebuilding the Roman Empire. In 531 the Byzantine Emperor Justinian concluded an 'Eternal Peace' with Rome's traditional rival, Persia, by paying 100,000lb of gold. This enabled him to turn west. Exploiting the outbreak of civil war among the Vandal rulers of North Africa, he sent out his commander Belisarius. With him were ninety-two *dromons* (a sort of light warship), 500 transports, and 15,000 troops excluding auxiliaries. This army was not the same as it had been in the days of ancient Rome. The legions had disappeared. The size of the units, and the role of infantry, had declined. Instead a critically important part was played by the cavalry, part of it heavy and part made up of horse archers, many of them barbarians.

Landing in Tunisia, Belisarius took the Vandals completely by surprise. First he routed them in the Battle of Ad Decimum, enabling him to capture Carthage. Next he defeated them at the larger Battle of Tricamarum. In both battles, the decisive factor was the behaviour of the Vandal King Gelimer who fled at the critical moment. Having conquered (though not completely pacified) Africa, Belisarius directed his attention to Sardinia, Corsica, the Balearics, and a stronghold near Gibraltar. All of these he occupied in a single campaign.

Belisarius' forces were always fairly small; he is credited with saying that 'not by numbers of men, nor by measure of body, but by valour of soul is war decided'.[*] Following his victories, he invaded Sicily with 7,500 men. From there, exploiting disagreements among the peninsula's Ostrogoth rulers, he marched northwards. Unable to take Rome, he bypassed it and captured Mediolanum (Milan) and the Ostrogoth capital Ravenna. At this point he was recalled by Justinian and sent to fight the Persians, who had broken the truce in the east, creating a diversion.

Belisarius' departure opened a decade of confused and very bloody fighting in Italy: it went first one way, then another, with Rome alone changing hands three times. Finally, in 552, Justinian was able to send out a force of 35,000 men under Belisarius' older colleague, Narses. Marching south from Ravenna, Narses met the Ostrogoths at Busta Gallorum and Mons Lactarius, in Etruria and near Mount Vesuvius respectively, defeating them and killing King Totila. Meanwhile a detachment of 2,000 men went to Spain where they occupied part of the south-eastern coast.

Justinian's military successes peaked in 555. At that time, except for the southern coasts of Gaul, the Mediterranean had again become a 'Roman' lake. But it did not last. In 568, two years after Justinian's death, Italy was lost to the Lombards. In the seventh century Africa and Spain followed.

---

[*] Quoted in P.K. Davis, *100 Decisive Battles* (Oxford: Oxford University Press, 1999), p. 93.

22

T'ang Campaigns Against the Eastern Turkic Kahganate

629

The Kahganate, made up of nomads who depended on camels for mobility in peace and war, had been subordinated by the T'ang Dynasty's predecessor, the Sui. The disturbances arising out of China's change of dynasty enabled it to become independent, but once that issue had been settled the new emperor, Taizong, decided to discipline what he saw as his rebellious subjects. His forces, commanded by General Li Jing, marched into what is now Inner Mongolia, where they surprised the enemy commander, Ashina Duobi, and almost succeeded in capturing him. Escaping at the last moment, Duobi withdrew to the Yin (or Daqing) Mountains, but was ultimately captured by the Chinese.

Typical of many, this campaign against the 'barbarians', though it ended in a Chinese victory, settled nothing. The outcome was twenty years of almost continuous warfare during which the nobility and people of the Kahganate alternately rebelled against Chinese rule and submitted to it. Repeatedly, Taizong sent out his daughters to marry Turkic chieftains; just as repeatedly, this device only helped preserve the peace up to a point. One solution envisaged by some of the emperor's

Emperor T'ang Taizong occupied Inner Mongolia, opening a series of conflicts that has lasted to the present day.

advisers was to uproot the Turkic people and resettle them south of the Yellow River. In fact a beginning was made on this enterprise, but it was never completed.

An interesting aspect of the wars, offering some parallels with the late Roman Empire, was the fact that Turkic forces served on both sides – under their own leaders as well as under T'ang command, as associates and mercenaries. In the end (649–50) it was a Chinese general of Turkic origin, Gao Kan, who defeated the Turkic leader Ashina Hubo and took him prisoner. After Taizong's death his successor, Gaozong, released Hubo and made him a general.

With that the attempt to rebuild the Kahganate ended, at least for the time being. This did not prevent subsequent Turkic generals from serving the emperor against some of their own people who had withdrawn west across the mountains into the Gobi Desert.

Mohammed's Followers Burst Out of the Arabian Peninsula

Twelve years after Mohammed had first proclaimed his new religion, and two years after his death, his followers burst out of the Arabian Peninsula. First, a host of 20,000, commanded by Khalid ibn al-Walid, defeated a Byzantine army of similar size in south-central Palestine. Next, after again beating the Byzantines at Yarmouk near the Sea of Galilee, they marched on Damascus, which they captured in 636.

From Syria, the Arabs with 30–40,000 men turned to Mesopotamia and Iran. If the sources may be believed, at al-Qādisiyyah in 636 they decisively defeated a Persian force two to three times as large. Having captured the Persian capital, Ctesiphon, they marched into Iran proper where in 642 they won another great battle, this time at Nahavand, near modern Hamadan. Contemporary Christian sources attribute these successes to God's wrath; Muslim ones, to Allah and the army's faith in him. Modern historians tend to think in terms of centuries of warfare between Persia and the Roman–Byzantine Empire, which left both sides exhausted.

Arab armies consisted of different kinds of heavy and light infantry and cavalry. Light cavalry, imaginatively used in skirmishing, feints, false retreats, and on the pursuit, was important. However, the decisive fighting always took place on foot. As Mohammed's son-in-law and successor, Ali ibn Abi

Talib, told his troops, it was a question of 'fighting with swords and staves, wrestling, biting and grappling'.[*] Much-needed engineering and siegecraft skills, which the Arabs initially lacked, were provided by renegades among the local population.

In 639, a Muslim army 70,000 strong invaded Egypt and won the Battle of Heliopolis. Next, meeting little resistance, it besieged one city after another until Alexandria capitulated in 642. From there they marched west. Carthage fell in 698, Tangier in 708. In 711 the Arabs took Gibraltar. Three times they tried to capture Constantinople by sea (654, 668–69, and 717–18). The first attempt was frustrated by a storm, the other two by the city's resistance using Greek fire.

Starting in 673, Arab–Muslim armies also moved east into Central Asia. The last major action in this theatre took place at Talas, on the border between Kazakhstan and Kyrgyzstan, in 751. The outnumbered Chinese suffered a crushing defeat, brought about mainly by the defection of their allies. Nevertheless, Talas marked the limit of Muslim expansion in this direction.

The Muslim surge remains an absolutely astonishing feat. Not only did the product – the Omayyad Empire – reach from the borders of China all the way to Spain, but almost all the countries it ruled have remained Muslim to the present day.

[*]   G.R. Hawting (trans.), *History of al-Tabari, Vol. 15, The First Civil War* (New York, NY: State University of New York Press, 1996), p. 30.

24

Battle of Tours Turns Back the Muslims in Europe

<u>732</u>

Twenty-one years after capturing Gibraltar, the Muslims (Moors) under Abd ar-Rahman reached Poitiers, in central France. There they were met by Charles Martel, a high official in the Frankish Merovingian administration who had made himself practically independent. Estimates of the strength on each side vary between 20,000 and 80,000. A more reasonable estimate might be 30,000, with the Christian Franks having the edge.

Having beaten Duke Odo of Aquitaine in the Battle of the Garonne earlier in the year, the 'plague of Saracens' (so called by the Carolingian chronicler Bede) infested southern France. However, the Arab commanders did not know that Martel was building another army to confront them. They were advancing in open order when they blundered into him. The two armies were not symmetrical. Whereas the Moors relied principally on cavalry, the most recent research indicates that Martel's force consisted mainly of heavy infantry. To enable them to withstand the Moorish cavalry he had them form a square. For seven days both sides confronted each other. In the end Abd ar-Rahman decided to attack; perhaps that was because winter, for which his troop were less well prepared than the Franks, was approaching fast.

Charles Martel ('The Hammer') put an end to the Muslim advance into Europe.

An outstanding characteristic of medieval warfare is that the cavalry normally had an edge over infantry. At Poitiers this was not yet the case, and Martel's experienced Franks stood their ground. As the *Mozarabic Chronicle* of 754, put it, 'the men of the North seemed like a sea that cannot be moved. Firmly they stood, one close to another, forming as it were a bulwark of ice.' Frankish sources claim that, just as the Moors broke into the square, a rumour spread that some enemy horsemen had broken into their camp, causing them to stop their attack so as to defend their loot. This enabled the Franks to recover. Trying to rally his men, Abd ar-Rahman was surrounded and killed. Frankish sources say that his forces disintegrated and fled, whereas Arab ones claim they were able to get away during the night.

Poitiers was not the end the struggle for France, which lasted for another twenty-seven years. But it did mark the high tide of the Muslims' northward advance.

25

In Europe the Shift Towards Cavalry Begins

c. 750

Late imperial Romans, Byzantines, Persians, Huns, and Arabs all depended heavily on cavalry of various kinds. Nevertheless, the most recent research tends to show that Charles Martel's Franks fought mainly on foot. So did earlier Franks and the Germanic peoples in general. At some point around 750, this started to change. The change may have been due to the introduction of the stirrup, first used in China during the fourth century and reaching Europe by way of the Middle East. Or perhaps it was not.

Be this as it may, the high middle ages were the age *par excellence* of heavy cavalry in particular. At some point after 1050 the riders adopted the classic technique of couching the lance. That is not to say that there were no other troops, such as spearmen, swordsmen, bowmen, crossbowmen, and later halberdiers. Not only did heavy cavalry always need escorts, but there were situations, such as sieges, in which cavalry was all but useless. When it came to the *guerre guerroyante*, the kind

Perhaps assisted by the invention of stirrups, the shift towards heavy armoured cavalry ('knights') began during the eighth century.

of warfare that did not involve pitched battles but skirmishing, raiding, and ravaging the countryside, light cavalry was often more useful than heavy. Nor does it mean that infantry never defeated cavalry. However, normally it could only do so in country that was unsuitable for the latter, either because it was swampy, as at Courtrai in 1302 and Crécy in 1346, or else because it was mountainous, as at Bannockburn in 1314 and Laupen in 1339.

There is no doubt that the dominance of heavy cavalry, made up of armoured knights, played a critically important role in shaping the middle ages. To some extent, the military, politics, society, and economics were all built around it – so much so that the 'age of chivalry' was named after it.

26

Beginning of Charlemagne's Wars

<u>771</u>

Charlemagne, the grandson of Charles Martel, ascended the Frankish throne in 768. In 771 he began his great campaign to conquer 'Saxony', meaning much of northern Germany east of the Rhine. The effort lasted thirty years before it finally succeeded, compelling the vanquished to submit to and accept Christianity.

One reason why it took so long was because Charlemagne was seldom able to concentrate on a single theatre of war. The years 773–74 found him in Italy, where he laid siege to the Lombard capital Pavia. Since the Franks had not brought along a siege train, the city had to be reduced by starvation, which took ten months. Meanwhile Saxony rose in revolt, forcing Charlemagne to return there in 776. A year later he led his troops across the Pyreneans to fight the Emir of Córdoba; but the expedition was a failure. It was during his retreat that there took place the incident at Roncesvalles, later immortalised in *La Chanson de Roland*.

Subsequent campaigns, some commanded by Charlemagne in person, took the Frankish armies to the Mediterranean. There they wrested Corsica and Sardinia from the Ostrogoths and took parts of south-eastern Spain from the Moors (779–812). They also put down a rebellion in Bretagne (786); occupied southern Italy (787); subdued Bavaria (787–88); conquered what is now Austria from the Avars; fought the Slavs east of the Elbe; invaded what is now Croatia; contested Dalmatia with the

Charlemagne. Some historians believe his armies were the most effective seen in Europe before Napoleon.

Byzantines (801–10); occupied Bohemia (805–06); and made war on the Danes, who had assisted the Saxon leader Widukind. Charlemagne's crowning achievement was the restoration of the 'Roman Empire' in the west in the year 800.

Little is known about the armies in question. Their core always consisted of Charlemagne's household troops. To this were added 'feudal' levies locally recruited by his subordinates, secular and ecclesiastical. Though the empire's total manpower resources may have enabled it to raise 100–120,000 men, whether Charlemagne ever concentrated more than 30,000 in any one theatre is doubtful. The sources provide glimpses concerning different kinds of cavalry and infantry as well as siege trains. Occupied districts were fortified and garrisoned. One historian has claimed that Charlemagne, illiterate though he and most of his subordinates were, 'commanded a planning staff and resources which may be compared favourably with what was to develop in Europe'[*] until the 1830s. Really?

---

[*] Bernard S. Bachrach, *Early Carolingian Warfare* (Philadelphia, PA: University of Philadelphia Press, 2001).

27

Beginning of the Viking Raids

789

Research having failed to uncover any clear motive behind the Viking raids, they present one of history's great riddles. All one can say is that, as the famous stories concerning the Valkyries and Valhalla (the place where dead warriors lived, made merry, and trained for the battle that would mark the end of the world) show, war was absolutely central to Viking life.

Great sailors and navigators, the Vikings reached their destinations by longboats: open vessels that relied on simple square sails. With their shallow draft, and by using oars, they could enter river mouths and make their way upstream. Originally the Vikings fought on foot, but upon arriving at their destinations they sometimes commandeered local horses for mobility. Weapons included bows, swords, spears, and battle axes; defensive equipment, helmets (round with peaked caps and nose guards, but without the horns so often associated with them), mail or scale armour, and round shields. During naval battles the shields were used to line the boats' sides so as to protect the crews against arrows. If the Vikings victims' accounts may be believed, though, their most important characteristic, which gave them their fearsome reputation, was their ferocity. Especially important were the *berserkers*, a group of warriors associated with the god Odin. Going into a sort of trance, they fought heedless of injury or the prospect of death.

The first to feel the impact of the raids were Scotland, England, and Ireland, where the Vikings raided, killed, burnt,

A ninth-century Viking warrior.

raped, looted, and settled, creating the so-called Danelaw in East Anglia. Later they reached Brittany and Normandy, as well as Aquitaine. Other parties – there never was a coordinated strategy – went further still. They raided the coasts of northern and western Spain, entered the Mediterranean, hit the coast of North Africa, and conquered Sicily and southern Italy. Some got as far as the Holy Land. Others entered Russia from the Baltic by way of the Great Rivers. They set up principalities and lorded it over the population of the Ukraine. Reaching Constantinople, they enlisted in the so-called Varangian Guard.

The Vikings' most important objective was always booty. However, they also settled certain areas, including Normandy, Iceland, and Greenland. Shortly before the year 1000, they even visited North America. Towards 1100 the Viking raids ceased almost as abruptly as they had begun, partly, apparently, because Europe's defences were improving, and partly because their countries of origin were being Christianised, causing some rulers to forego raiding in favour of crusading.

28

Beginning of the Hungarian Campaigns in Europe

<u>894</u>

The Hungarian tribes' original home was east of the Urals. Participating in the great migration of peoples, not long after 800 they allied themselves with the Bulgarians in fighting the Byzantine Empire. In 896, united under a tribal leader by the name of Árpád, they crossed the Carpathians and settled in what has since been known as the Hungarian Plain.

The Hungarian way of war was typical of Asian nomadic peoples. The men fought mounted with the composite bow as their principal weapon; operationally, the key elements were speed and well-coordinated manoeuvre. Driving west, in 907 20,000 Hungarians are said to have utterly destroyed a Bavarian army three times their strength at the Battle of Pressburg (Bratislava). From there they moved to Augsburg where, in 910, they defeated Louis the Child, the last legitimate surviving prince of the German branch of the house of Charlemagne. Taking advantage of the Viking raids, they in turn raided west through modern Saxony, Alsace, Switzerland, and Burgundy. Even Spain felt the impact, which was every bit as bad as that of the Huns five centuries earlier.

Hungarian westward expansion was brought to an end by the Battle of Lechfeld in 955. A Hungarian force, said to have been 20,000 strong, was besieging Augsburg. At that time a Frankish–German army under Otto the Great, King of East Francia, came up to relieve the city with a force only one-third as large. Thanks to the Danube, which was behind the Hungarians, the latter's light cavalry had no room to manoeuvre and the west European heavy cavalry was able to catch up with it. Next, when they tried to put into effect their favourite tactic of the feigned retreat, Otto's men were not tempted to pursue. Instead they rigorously maintained their battle order, systematically slaughtering their enemies.

The battle brought the Hungarians' westward advance to an abrupt end. However, for the next two centuries they kept pressing southward in the direction of Croatia until they were finally defeated and brought to a halt by the Byzantines in the Battle of Sirmium (1167), in today's Serbia.

29

Urban II Proclaims the First Crusade

<u>1095</u>

It was to loud applause that Pope Urban II (*Deus lo vult*, it is God's wish) proclaimed the First Crusade. Four crusader hosts, made up predominantly of Frenchmen of all social classes and numbering perhaps 30–35,000 in all, left in August 1096. Taking different routes through what are now southern Germany, Austria, Hungary, and the Balkans, they met at Constantinople. From there they went to Nicaea, in Asia Minor, which they besieged and, with Byzantine help, captured. Next, proceeding east in the summer of 1097, they were caught at a disadvantage by the Sultan of Rûm, Kilij Arslan, and almost annihilated in the Battle of Dorylaeum.

Recovering in the nick of time, in May 1098 the Crusaders besieged and captured Antioch, in Syria, by treachery. A year later still, commanded by Raymond of Toulouse and Godfrey of Bouillon, and assisted by a Genoese fleet that provided supplies, engineers, and the wherewithal to build siege engines, they took Jerusalem, which they subjected to a horrible bloodbath. By that time perhaps only a third of the original force was left, the rest having perished on the way. Yet that very summer the Crusader army met a Saracen force twice its size coming up from Egypt at Ascalon, on the Mediterranean shore, and defeated it.

The Crusade led to the establishment of three small feudal states: Edessa, Antioch, and Jerusalem. The outcome was prolonged, if sporadic, fighting between Crusaders and

A mounted crusader.

Saracens. Most of it consisted of skirmishes, raids, and sieges rather than battles. Highlights were the Second Crusade, started in 1147 in response to the fall of the county of Edessa; the Battle of Hattin in 1187, in which the Crusaders suffered a crushing defeat, enabling the Saracen commander Saladin to capture Jerusalem in the same year; the launch of the Third Crusade, led by the most famous Crusader of all, Richard Lionheart, in 1189; the Fourth Crusade, which led to the sack of Constantinople in 1204; and the fifth, which foundered in Egypt in 1221.

From start to finish the Crusaders, thanks to their alliances with Genoa and Venice, held the advantage at sea. On land, though, initially the two sides were asymmetrical. The Crusaders relied mainly on heavy cavalry, the Saracens on light. However, in time they started learning from each other and in many ways became more alike. Both sides also deployed infantry, including bowmen and crossbowmen, as well as siege engines. The end came in 1291 when the last Crusader stronghold at Château Pèlerin, south of Haifa, fell to the Mamluk Sultan Al-Ashraf Khalil. It was caused more by the Saracens' numerical advantage than any other factor.

30

Opening of Genghis Khan's Campaigns

1197

Genghis' rise to power began in 1186 when, following an enormously complicated series of wars, espionage, intrigues, and murders, the assembly of Mongol tribal chieftains elected him *Khan* (chief). By 1197 he had also subjected neighbouring tribes, such as Naimans, the Merkits, and the Tanguts. By 1206 he ruled the entire Mongolian plain.

At this point Genghis started his spectacular career as a conqueror. First he defeated the Xia in north-western China. Next it was the turn of the Jin Dynasty in Manchuria. At the Battle of Huan'erzui in 1211, 90,000 Mongols took on a much larger Jin force and annihilated it. The Jin capital Yanjing (Beijing) fell in 1215. In 1232, five years after Genghis' death, its fate was shared by the alternative capital, Kaifeng.

Having conquered China, the Mongols under one of Genghis' grandsons, Batu Khan, turned west. During the late 1230s they overran the 'Rus' principalities in the Ukraine. In 1241 they defeated the Poles and the Hungarians at the battles of Liegnitz and Mohi respectively, opening the way into Austria and the Adriatic shore. Batu Khan was besieging Buda when Ögedei Khan, Genghis' third son, died, forcing Batu to return home so as to contest the imperial throne.

In 1244 a Mongol host marched through northern Persia and Kurdistan and was threatening Syria. Possibly because they had no siege train with them, they were forced to withdraw.

Genghis Khan created the largest empire that ever was.

However, in 1255, first under Genghis' grandson Hulagu and then under his former assistant Kitbuqa Noyan (a Nestorian Christian, incidentally), they returned. First they captured and thoroughly sacked Baghdad, killing the last Abbasid caliph and ending the 'golden age' of Islamic culture. Next, in 1260, they marched to Ein Jalud, in the Esdraelon valley. There they faced a vastly superior Mamluk army under the Sultan of Egypt, Baibars, and were soundly defeated.

Made up of men accustomed to the saddle almost from birth, the highly mobile Mongol armies consisted largely of light cavalry, armed with composite bows, spears and sabres. Later some infantry and engineers, many of them non-Mongols, were added. The armies were divided into decimal units – 10, 100, 1,000, and 10,000 strong – and kept in touch with each other by way of fast relay systems. Their favourite tactic was the feigned retreat, followed by a turnaround and an advance in two 'horns' to encircle the enemy. The outcome was the largest empire in history, including China, Central Asia, much of Russia and the Ukraine, as well as parts of Persia and modern Iraq. 'As far as their horses' hooves can carry them,' as the saying went.

31

First Mongol Attempt to Invade Japan

1274

Kublai Khan, a grandson of the great Genghis, became Emperor of China in 1260. Six years later, claiming to have 'the mandate of heaven', he sent a letter to the 'king of Japan' demanding submission and tribute. Not receiving an answer, he sent additional emissaries but was rebuffed every time. In 1271 he decided to invade.

Three years later the expedition, consisting of an estimated 600–700 vessels (300 large, the rest smaller) and some 23,000 Chinese and Korean troops, set out and carried out several landings on Kyushu, Japan's south-western island closest to Korea. Japan at the time had been at peace for several decades. Perhaps that is why the Mongol troops enjoyed clear technological superiority in the form of short composite bows, firecrackers, and ceramic grenades. Known in Chinese as 'thunder-crash bombs', the latter were filled with explosives and thrown at the enemy by means of catapults.

Some of the battles that developed on the beachheads went in favour of the Mongols, others not. The decisive factor was a typhoon that destroyed some 200 Mongol ships. Thereupon the samurai, carried by the smaller, nimbler Japanese ships, made use of the darkness to approach the larger Mongol vessels. They boarded them and overcame their crews in ferocious hand-to-hand fighting.

A Mongol warrior.

In 1281, after several more diplomatic attempts to make Japan submit had failed, Kublai Khan tried again. This time the forces he sent were much larger, allegedly consisting of two fleets with 4,400 ships and 140,000 troops between them. Again the objective was Kyushu where several landings were attempted. However, the Japanese had used the interval to fortify the relevant beaches. That was why, on the whole, they succeeded in repelling the invaders even though they were outnumbered. Another factor was that, to save money, the Mongols used many ships that, being small and flat-bottomed, were unsuitable for the open sea, leading to numerous losses.

Subsequent Chinese rulers also demanded that Japan surrender. However, the failure of these two expeditions saved the country from being occupied. So it remained until 1945, when it surrendered to the US following the dropping of two atomic bombs.

32

Outbreak of the Hundred Years War

1337

The background to this conflict was the claim of Edward III of England to the French throne, after Charles IV of France died without male issue. Matters were complicated by the fact that, for the territory of Aquitaine, Edward was the vassal of France's new king, Philip VI. Claiming that Edward had neglected his duties as a vassal, Charles confiscated Aquitaine, thereby opening the war.

In June 1340 an English fleet decisively defeated a French one at Sluys, giving the English command of the Channel for the rest of the war. The two sides spent the next five years contesting Brittany, where civil war had broken out and many cities passed from hand to hand. The first major battle was fought at Crécy in 1346. Having raided the environs of Paris, the English marched back to the Pas-de-Calais. They were cornered by the numerically superior French and forced to make a stand. As the French knights charged, they were decimated by the English longbowmen. Two other battles, those of Poitiers (1356) and Agincourt (1415), were fought along broadly similar lines and led to similar results. The second of these was all but decisive, leading to the marriage of Henry V with the French princess Catherine of Valois on the understanding that their offspring would inherit the French throne.

It was not to be. In 1429 the French, inspired by Joan of Arc ('*la puella*', as she was known), relieved the siege of Orléans.

An English longbowman.

Joan herself was captured by the Burgundians, who sold her to their English allies. In turn, the English burnt her at the stake. However, the war went on and French successes, greatly assisted by newly developed siege artillery, multiplied. A decisive moment was formed by the Battle of Castillon, in Gascony, in 1453. Leaving the French masters of the field, it forced the English to evacuate the whole of France except Calais.

Though interrupted by several truces, the war was enormously destructive. And all the more so because, having begun as feudal conflict, for much of the time it was also a French civil war fought by the magnates for the possession of cities and provinces. Freebooters (*écorcheurs* in French) joined the struggle, looting, burning, and killing. The war also witnessed many technological innovations, especially in the field of firearms, which went a long way to render armoured knights obsolete. Above all, by the time hostilities ended what started as a dynastic conflict had developed into a war between two quite distinct national countries.

33

First Recorded Use of Gunpowder in the West

1346

Known to the Arabs as 'Chinese snow', gunpowder had been known in China for centuries. From there it spread to India, Central Asia, and Europe by way of the Mediterranean.

Early gunpowder weapons took the form of firecrackers, probably meant more to terrify than to hurt. They also included variously shaped explosive ceramic containers hurled from catapults. Genghis Khan, employing Chinese experts, used them in Central Asia. The question of gunpowder's development is complicated by the fact that the terminology is not always clear. At times gunpowder was confused with various kinds of incendiaries, including Greek fire. The latter, a somewhat mysterious substance that would burn on water, was repeatedly used by the Byzantines against the Arabs in particular. Often it is hard to say what device the sources are referring to. Illustrations, some apparently by men who had never seen a firearm, are not always helpful either.

Cannon were used at Crécy in 1346. By 1400 two main kinds of firearms – crew-operated and hand-held – had become distinct. Most were muzzle-loaders, though here and there experiments were made with breech-loaders as well. Used both in the field and for siege warfare, both for offense and for defence, firearms steadily gained in importance. Especially critical turning points were the invention, around 1430, of corned powder, which

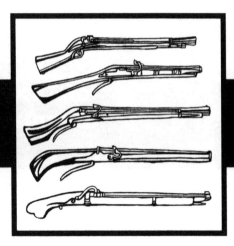

Some early handguns.

greatly increased the energy delivered per pound of weight; the Ottoman capture of Constantinople in 1453, brought about with the aid of a 63cm-calibre gun firing stone balls; and the Battle of Pavia in 1525, said to be the first in European history decided by arquebus-carrying (Spanish) infantry.

By 1600 European firearms, large and small, were outclassing all the rest. However, some societies and armies rejected gunpowder for domestic reasons. The outcome was defeat, such as when the Mamluks failed to stop the Ottomans from conquering Palestine and Egypt in 1517, or military irrelevance, as in the case of the Japanese samurai under Tokugawa rule from 1603 on. Nomadic peoples also found it hard to manufacture, though not to use, firearms. As a result, their days of glory passed and they found themselves increasingly helpless.

Gunpowder continued in use until the early 1880s, when it was replaced by smokeless powder. Though not the only factor, its role in bringing about European domination of the world cannot be overestimated.

34

Opening of Timur's Campaigns

1370

Timur (meaning 'Iron'), then probably in his late thirties, was a Turco-Mongol. He gained control of the western Chagatai Khanate, a vast area in Central Asia previously ruled by a descendant of Genghis Khan. His campaigns mark the last time a nomadic civilisation was able to overcome settled ones on a large scale.

Timur's conquests were carried out in the name of Islam on one hand and the Mongol heritage on the other. He spent the 1370s campaigning west of the Caspian. In 1381 he tackled Persia. He captured Tehran, which, having surrendered, was leniently treated, and thoroughly sacked the rebellious city of Isfizar, where live prisoners were cemented into a wall. He also had 150–200,000 citizens of Isfahan massacred and twenty-eight towers, made of 1,500 skulls each, erected. Sources describe his troops systematically herding together and raping the female population as if they were doing fatigue duty.

In 1385 Timur, attacked by the Golden Horde in the north, interrupted his westward advance. Instead he marched into Russia with 100,000 men, proceeding far enough for them to complain that the long summer days interfered with the schedule of five daily prayers. In 1395, having defeated the Horde in the Battle of Terek River, he turned south. Passing through Afghanistan, in 1398 he took Delhi where another 100,000 prisoners were massacred.

In 1399 Timur resumed his march westward. First he invaded Armenia and Georgia, then, in 1401, he sacked Aleppo and Damascus. In 1402 he defeated and captured Sultan Bayezid, leading to a temporary pause in Ottoman expansion. Later the English playwright Christopher Marlowe made a great play of this by showing 'Tamburlaine' keeping Bayezid in a cage, feeding him scraps, and using him as a footstool, until he killed himself onstage by bashing in his head.

Timur's victims must have numbered in the millions. His last campaigns (1404–05) were directed against Ming China but were halted by his death. The core of Timur's armies was formed by the usual Asiatic horse archers, who were capable of fighting on foot as well. He also had captives and renegades from among subject peoples who built and operated his siege engines. Indeed, it is said that whenever he sacked a city he spared the well-educated. If this is true, then it would indicate that his massacres, like his rapes, were well planned, systematic, and orderly.

35

Dmitry Donskoy Defeats the Golden Horde at Kulikovo

1380

The battle, on the Don not far from Tula, marks the beginning of the Muscovite struggle for independence from the Golden Horde, as Batu Khan's Mongol successors in the regions north of the Black Sea were known.

The background was formed by Timur's campaigns to the south, which had distracted the Horde and weakened it. The Tartar commander was Mamai, who ruled southern and eastern Ukraine as well as the Crimea. The Muscovite one was Prince Dmitry Donskoy, who had assembled a league of Russian principalities. The Tartars, descendants of the armies of Genghis Khan, were armed and organised according to their traditional system, which centred on horse archers (whether they also used firearms is moot). Very little is known about the Muscovite armies, except that they consisted of infantry as well as cavalry, wore curious pointed helmets, and either hauberks or scale armour (at least the officers and better-off troops did), and were armed with bows and spears. The Russian force probably numbered about 60,000, whereas the Tartar one may have been twice as large.

Very little is known about the battle except that it started at about eleven o'clock after the morning mist had cleared. First there took place a single combat between champions – a custom often observed among the Mongols and their enemies.

On this occasion both champions are said to have been killed; but whereas the Russian one remained stuck in the saddle, his Tartar opponent did not. Next the Tartars attacked the Muscovite centre. However, the latter held steady until Prince Bobrok, Dmitry's cousin, at the head of a cavalry force hit them in the flank. If the sources may be believed, almost all the Tartars present became casualties, making this one of the bloodiest encounters in history. Muscovite casualties amounted to 20,000.

The battle was the opening shot in a long series of wars, which went now one way, now another. It only came to an end in 1552 when Ivan IV ('The Terrible') led a 150,000-strong Muscovite army towards Kazan. Laying siege to the city, the Russians used a tower, mines, and no fewer than 150 artillery pieces to achieve their aim. This was a relatively modern force that the Tartars, whose methods of life and war had remained basically unchanged for almost three centuries, could not resist. At the end of two months the city fell, after which its fortifications were demolished and much of its population was massacred.

36

Opening of the Aztec Imperial Wars

1427

The first war, waged against the Tepanec tribe by the Mexica and Acolhua, ended in 1428 with the establishment of the Triple Alliance between the three tribes. That alliance, in turn, became the basis of the Aztec Empire.

Like the Romans, one of whose traditions traced back their origins to the war god Mars, the Aztecs were a warrior people through and through. The usual power, wealth, and glory apart, the objective of their warfare was to obtain captives for sacrifice. Young men started training when they reached their fifteenth birthday. The standing army was limited to the imperial household troops; the rest would be mobilised as necessary. Nobles and commoners apparently served in separate units, but warfare provided a ladder for social ascent: the more enemies a soldier had captured, the higher his rank. Armies up to 700,000-men strong, including many porters (the Aztecs had neither beasts of burden nor made use of the wheel for carriage), are mentioned. But these figures seem as exaggerated as Herodotus' claim that Xerxes led 2.5 million men to Greece.

Weapons consisted of spears, swords, daggers, darts, slings, bows, and blowguns. As the Aztecs had only just started to work metal, all these were made of wood and fibre with sharp obsidian edges, and the occasional copper point. Defensive apparel included leather or quilted cotton armour, wooden helmets, and shields. Discipline was strict and marching performances compared favourably with those of other armies.

Geographically isolated, the Aztecs developed a unique style of war.

'Strategic' communications were maintained by way of smoke and fire signals, as well as runners on foot; tactical orders were transmitted by voice and a variety of musical instruments. An Aztec army would start a battle with fire from bows and slings before engaging in melee. Favourite manoeuvres included the envelopment and the false retreat, followed by an ambush.

Opinions about the effectiveness of Aztec warfare were and remain divided. It certainly enabled the Aztecs to build an empire, which, at its peak, occupied some 150,000sq. km in central Mexico. It also brought in thousands of prisoners annually for sacrifice to the gods. In the words of the Spanish friar Diego Durán, Aztec rulers 'conquered all the nations'. With an estimated 11 million subjects, they made themselves 'masters of the world'.[*] Other Spanish accounts emphasise the Aztecs' courage, determination, and ferocity. Yet they also emphasise the 'childish' nature of their warfare, which enabled a mere handful of *conquistadores* to subdue them in 1519. The question is unlikely to receive a definitive answer.

[*] D. Duran, *The History of the Indies of New Spain* (Norman, OK: University of Oklahoma Press, 1994), p. 336.

37

Opening of the Inca Imperial Wars

1438

L ike the Aztecs, the Incas were just beginning to work metal when the European invasion curtailed their development. Also like the Aztecs, they were a military people accustomed to regimentation, strict discipline, and warfare, but they built vast fortifications more regularly than the Aztecs. They also set up an extensive road system and maintained an elaborate logistic system assisted by a native form of writing, *quipu*. These systems enabled them to rule an empire which, at its peak, extended over 800,000sq. km with a population of perhaps 20 million.

Inca topography differed greatly from that of the Aztecs. Furthermore, the two civilisations had little or no contact. Nevertheless, their weapons and tactics were quite similar. To them the Inca added the bola, a throwing weapon made of weights on the ends of interconnected cords. Armies could be up to 100,000 strong, though that number probably refers to all the disposable forces rather than to individual field armies.

Like the Aztecs, the Inca developed a style of war all their own. Like the Aztecs, they were defeated by the Spanish *conquistadores*.

Unlike the Aztecs, the Incas did not ritually sacrifice large numbers of prisoners (enemies were hung by their hair and left for the condors to devour). They did, however, sometimes uproot defeated peoples and settle them in other districts of their empire.

From 1438 on, the string of Inca victories was almost unbroken. Yet in 1533 they too were conquered by a handful of enterprising Spaniards. In both cases what made the Europeans' victory possible was the defection of the ruling people's allies as well as their own technological superiority. Above all, there was the sheer daring and ruthlessness displayed by the Spanish commanders and men which, in retrospect, appear almost incredible.

38 The Ottomans Capture Constantinople

In 1299 Osman I announced his independence from the Seljuk Sultanate of Rûm, starting the Ottomans' great march of conquest. Eventually it brought the whole of Anatolia, Syria, Mesopotamia, Arabia, the Balkans, and North Africa under his descendants' control.

Osman's men were known as Ghazis, an Arab term meaning either 'raiders' or 'holy warriors'. Illustrations show them armed with the usual light cavalrymen's weapons, i.e. composite bow, spear, and sword. With them he advanced against the Byzantine Empire, reaching both the Sea of Marmora and the Aegean Sea in 1308.

In 1321 the Ottomans, crossing the Aegean for the first time, landed in Thrace. Advancing north, they went on to defeat the Serb and Bulgarian empires in the battles of Kosovo (1389) and Nicopolis (1396) respectively. They also invaded Albania where, however, they faced tough resistance that only ended in the 1450s. Their greatest victory came in 1453 when, following five earlier failed attempts, they finally took Constantinople. The siege lasted fifty-three days. It was conducted both by land and by sea with the aid of forces variously estimated at 50–300,000 men under Sultan Mehmed II. He used seventy artillery pieces, the heaviest of which were apparently built and operated by Hungarian renegades.

Starting in 1386, the core of the obviously very effective Ottoman armies consisted of the janissaries. Numbering a few

At peak, Ottoman armies were among the most effective in the world.

tens of thousands, they were full-time, salaried slave soldiers recruited while still very young (7–12 years of age) from among Christian communities in the Balkans and the Caucasus. A larger number of troops, known as timar after the plots of land they received under a kind of feudal arrangement, were part time. Arms and equipment, firearms included, were as good as any available in Eurasia during the period in question. Fleets, often consisting of hundreds of galleys, were provided and operated by the populations of conquered coastal provinces. They ranged throughout the Mediterranean, fought their Venetian, Genoan, and Spanish opponents on equal terms, and raided and occasionally obtained footholds as far west as Catalonia.

The capture of Constantinople did not end the run of Ottoman success. Besides conquering Rhodes in 1522, they also overran modern Romania, Croatia, and Slovenia. In 1526 they crushed the Hungarian nobility in the Battle of Mohács, opening the way to Vienna itself. Not to mention other Ottoman armies that, during the period here discussed, reached the frontiers of India, overran the Crimea and the Caucasus, and conquered North Africa.

39

Dawning of the Columbian Age

c. 1460

Ancient Greek and Roman navies consisted of galleys. In battle they were propelled by oars, but for general navigation they relied on sails. Medieval navies were made up of cogs, also known as roundships: single-masted vessels with square sails that were not specialised for either trade or war. Neither of these types nor the ships various seafaring peoples built for the Ottomans were suitable for long oceanic voyages. As the expeditions of Admiral Zheng He between 1405 and 1433 showed, the largest Chinese ships, known as junks, could and did make such voyages. However, their owners preferred to fight them with the aid of troops carrying edged weapons rather than with artillery.

The first to build full-rigged ships were the Portuguese. Known as carracks, they had rounded sterns, curved sides, elevated bowsprits, and aftcastles, and two to five masts carrying various kinds of sails. Increasingly they were equipped with gun ports. Starting as early as 1421, such ships enabled the Portuguese under Henry the Navigator (a name, incidentally, he was only given much later) to explore the Atlantic, where they reached Madeira, the Azores, and the Cape Verdes. They also sailed south, reaching the Cape of Good Hope in 1488 and India in 1498.

These voyages were unopposed. However, east of the Cape the Portuguese command of the sea was contested first by

A galleon of the kind that enabled Charles V to rule the Empire over which the sun never set.

various Arab rulers along Asia's southern shores and later by Indian princes. In their attempts to stop the Portuguese, on occasion Arabs and Indians formed coalitions. The naval struggle waged between the two sides from 1505 onwards went both ways. However, in 1509 the Battle of Chaul, off the Indian port of Diu, settled the issue in favour of the Portuguese.

The Portuguese efforts focused on wresting the highly profitable spice trade away from the Venetians who used the Egyptian route to India. Meanwhile a Spanish expedition, hoping to reach India from the east and vastly underestimating the distances involved, discovered America. Towards the end of the sixteenth century the sailors of both nations were joined and overtaken by those of England, France, and, above all, the Netherlands. Though still not specialised for either trade or war, by this time so superior were the European ocean-going ships, such as the Spanish galleons and the Dutch and English East Indiamen, that their command of the sea was well nigh absolute. From then on, for several centuries, the only important naval battles at sea were those fought between opposing European fleets.

40

Completion of the *Reconquista*

Having crossed the Straits of Gibraltar in 711, by 719 the Arabs had defeated the Visigoths and overrun the entire Iberian Peninsula. As early as 722, though, a rebellion got under way in Asturias – one that the Muslims, owing to the mountainous terrain that favoured guerrilla warfare, could never quite overcome. The local Christian commander Pelagius (Pelayo) founded a dynasty that gradually expanded his kingdom's borders until it covered all of north-western Iberia. The regions freed of Moorish rule saw the establishment of any number of minor kingdoms, the last of which were only united towards the very end of the struggle in 1492.

Warfare in Spain differed from that further north. Light cavalry played a greater role, heavy cavalry a smaller one. However, as time went by the latter gained in importance. The infantry, armed with swords, and bows, and wearing light if any armour, were known as *peones*, a name that speaks for itself. From about 1400 on, growing use was made of firearms. Numbers were generally small, hardly ever exceeding 30,000 on either side.

The principal turning points were as follows. In 834 (or 844) Ramiro I of Asturias defeated the Muslims in the legendary

Battle of Clavijo, earning the apostle Saint James, who suddenly appeared and inspired the Christians, his title of Santiago Matamoros (Moor-Slayer). This was followed by war in Navarre, which gained its independence in 1002. In 1035 Aragón did the same, continuing to expand south until it reached its present borders in 1285. Lisbon, capital of Portugal, fell in 1147 after the pope had directed a Crusade against its Moorish owners. Yet progress was anything but easy. For example, in 1195 Alfonso VIII of Castile, one of the newly established Christian kingdoms, was defeated in the so-called Disaster of Alarcos.

In 1211 a new Moorish army under Mohammed al-Nasir crossed from Africa, causing Pope Innocent III to proclaim another Crusade. A year later French, Navarrese, Aragónese, Castilian, and Portuguese forces, commanded by Sancho VII of Navarre, inflicted a heavy defeat on the Moors at Las Navas de Tolosa.

By that time Moorish control was limited to the southern third of the peninsula. The last major battle between Christians and Moors was fought at Rio Saldo in 1340, after which only Granada remained in Moorish hands. Gibraltar was captured in 1469, and in 1492 Granada fell to the united forces of Ferdinand of Aragón and Isabella of Castile.

Part III

FIGHTING WITH GUNS

1495–1815 CE

Opening of the Italian Wars

<u>1494</u>

The Italian Wars began when France's Charles VIII, at the head of 25,000 men of whom 8,000 were Swiss mercenaries, marched into Italy. Advancing '*col gesso*' (chalk in hand, i.e. easily), as Machiavelli says, he headed for Naples where he established a pro-French regime. On his way back he easily defeated a league of Italian states at Fornovo, thus exposing their utter weakness.

From this point on Italy became a battlefield. French, Spanish, and Austrian–German armies struggled for control over the peninsula, whereas the Italian states were reduced to playing a secondary role at best. From 1519 on, with Spain and the empire united under Charles V, the struggle also embraced Provence, Alsace, Lorraine, the Low Countries, and north-western France.

Most of the troops were mercenaries. Over time the role of heavy cavalry declined, whereas that of infantry increased. Particularly important in this respect were the Swiss *Haufen* which, fighting under their own commanders, often switched sides according to whether or not they were paid; the German *Landsknechte*, who were modelled after them; and, above all, the Spanish *tercios*. All these started as heavy phalanxes made up of pikemen. Later they were joined by arquebusiers who protected their flanks. Cooperation with artillery, now made mobile by being provided with wheeled carriages, and with cavalry, which increasingly discarded the lance and took up pistols instead, was vital.

European armour peaked around 1525, after which it began to be discarded stage by stage.

Waged intermittently with many interruptions, the wars were punctuated by a large number of extremely bloody battles. Among the most important were those of Ravenna (1512), where the French crushed the Spaniards; Novara (1513), where the Swiss defeated the French; Marignano (1515) where the French overcame the Swiss; the Battle of Pavia (1525) in which Charles V defeated the French and took King Francis I prisoner; the sack of Rome by Charles' troops (1527); and the Battle of Marciano (1554) in which the Spaniards beat the French. Yet the decisive encounter was fought not in Italy but at St-Quentin, in modern Belgium, in 1557. There a combined Spanish–Savoyard army inflicted a crushing defeat on the French, leading to the Peace of Cateau-Cambrésis two years later.

The wars left north and south Italy in Spanish hands, with the papal state uneasily sandwiched in between. In retrospect, they heralded the struggle between France and the Habsburg Empire which, proceeding in one guise or another, only ended in 1918 or even 1945.

42
Introduction of the Artillery Fortress

c. 1522

Starting in prehistoric times, fortresses and city walls had always been built as tall as possible so as to make them hard to scale. As artillery grew in power after 1450, though, breaching such fortifications became relatively easy. The new fortresses represented an attempt to correct this problem.

The secret of making fortifications immune to cannon rounds was to build them *into* the ground. A combination of long, straight walls with squat, wedged towers (bastions) permitted the entire length of the surrounding moat, as well as the glacis on the other side of it, to be raked by the defenders' guns. The latter were either located in special embrasures or else mounted atop the low, flat walls. Furthermore, to enable the bastions to protect not only the walls but each other, they were arranged in symmetrical order, with blunt angles projecting outward in every direction. This created the characteristic star-like fortifications, hundreds of which were to dot the European countryside. Later some also blocked the river mouths along America's eastern shores.

To capture the new fortifications, it was necessary, first, to build lines of vallation and countervallation; second, dig trenches, place cannon in them, and drive the defenders off the nearby walls; third, dig another trench, closer to the wall, and repeat the process; fourth, dig yet another trench, closer still; fifth, create what was called 'a practical breach'; and sixth, in case the defenders did not surrender, storm the city.

By using such methods, and given enough time, in principle any fortress could be captured. But the engineers responsible for the defence did not resign themselves to the growing power of artillery. Instead they responded by adding so-called outworks to present the attacker with successive fortified belts. Over time those belts became fantastically elaborate as ravelins, redoubts, bonnettes, lunettes, tenailles, and countless other structures were added.

Thus, contrary to the common wisdom, siege warfare did not become easier nor sieges shorter. Instead both fortifications and artillery grew larger, more powerful, and more expensive, causing the number of those who could afford them to decline. The outcome was greater political centralisation. Down to the end of the eighteenth century, sieges were at least as numerous as battles. As late as the 1830s, the works of the greatest engineer of all, Sébastien le Prestre de Vauban (1633–1707), who specialised both in building fortifications and capturing them, remained in print and were used as practical guides.

43

The Battle of Lepanto

1571

The Mongols and Arabs having been repulsed, by this time the only remaining power capable of challenging Western Europe was the Ottoman Empire. Indeed one reason why the series of wars that started in 1494 lasted as long as it did was because Emperor Charles V and his successors had to cope not only with France but with the Ottomans too. After 1562, though, France sank into civil war, freeing the hands of Charles' son, Philip II of Spain, in particular.

In 1565 the Ottomans suffered a major reverse as their attempt to capture Malta, made with 193 ships and 48,000 troops, ended in failure. Five years later Venice, Genoa, Spain, and the Pope formed an alliance to try to save the Venetian garrison in Cyprus, which was being attacked by a large Ottoman force. The Christian commander was John of Austria, an illegitimate son of Charles V. The fleet, consisting of 212 ships with 40,000 sailors and oarsmen, and 28,000 fighting troops on board, reached the Gulf of Patras in October 1571. There they encountered the Ottoman fleet with 280 ships, 13,000 sailors, 37,000 oarsmen (almost all slaves), and 34,000 fighting troops. On both sides, galleys formed the vast majority of all ships.

The Christians' main advantage was their artillery – they had 1,815 guns to the Ottomans' 750 – but also the personal firearms

they carried (the Ottomans used bows). Each fleet formed a line running from north to south. The outcome was a series of complex, rather uncoordinated, manoeuvres punctuated by wild melees. This enabled the Christian galleasses (relatively large ships capable of carrying more artillery than galleys could) to prove themselves. So did the excellent Spanish infantry, fighting hand to hand. When the battle ended the Ottomans had lost no fewer than 210 ships, many of them captured in sufficiently good condition to be reused by the victors. Christian losses were limited to twenty ships, plus thirty damaged beyond repair. Casualties on the Ottoman side were also much higher – the more so because, in the battle's aftermath, a great many Christian galley slaves were liberated.

This outcome did not prevent the Ottomans from taking Cyprus in 1572. The Porte soon rebuilt his ships; however, finding good crews for them proved difficult and the fleet never recovered. Most historians consider the battle as the beginning of the end of Ottoman attempts to dominate the Mediterranean.

44

The Battle of Nagashino

The Battle of Nagashino marked a fresh outbreak of armed struggles between various Japanese *daimyo* (warlords) while at the same time introducing modern warfare into the country.

Previously Japanese warfare had been rather primitive: firearms were all but unknown, and many battles opened with duels between individual champions. In 1543 some Portuguese personnel, having suffered shipwreck, introduced arquebuses. Soon enough the Japanese started copying them and producing them by the thousand. At Nagashino some 3,000 newly raised arquebusiers enabled Oda Nobunaga, governor of Owari Province, to rout the troops of one of his rivals who were still using the old arms and relying on the old tactics, including a cavalry charge.

As in Europe, firearms were combined with pikemen fighting in dense formation. As in Europe, too, the fact that firearms did not demand much skill in use caused them to be regarded as low-class weapons. Meanwhile, the samurai stuck to their traditional swords, bows and arrows. Expanding in scale and sophistication, Japanese warfare consisted of raids, skirmishes, and battles that were punctuated by more or less prolonged sieges.

As civil war raged, particularly important in this respect was Ishiyama Hongan-ji, an enormous fortress near Osaka which was staffed by warrior monks. Amidst an endlessly complicated series of military actions, Oda Nobunaga conquered most of the islands of Honshu and Kyushu, enabling him to take a shot at his real objective in all these struggles: the Shogunate. However, in 1582 he was killed by one of his own deputies, whereupon leadership of his clan passed to Toyotomi Hideyoshi.

In 1590 Hideyoshi, now in command of no fewer than 170,000 men, took the fortress of Odawar, in southern Honshu, thereby all but unifying Japan. Twice he sent expeditions to invade Korea, but his troops were unable to prevail against Korean and Chinese opposition. In 1598 he died and was succeeded by Tokugawa Ieyasu. Ieyasu in turn proved more than a match for Hideyoshi's other generals, defeating them at the Battle of Sekigahara in 1600, in which firearms again played a decisive role.

Having become Shogun, Ieyasu closed the country to foreigners, had the Christians among the population executed, and disarmed the peasantry. He also founded a dynasty that lasted until 1868, and under which Japan fought hardly any wars, either foreign or domestic.

45

Defeat of the Spanish Armada

1588

At this time Spain, sustained by a mighty flow of silver from America, was probably the most powerful single country in the world – the more so because it ruled Portugal and its empire as well. However, Spanish hegemony was challenged by Dutch Protestant rebels, who were assisted by their co-religionist Queen Elizabeth I of England. The English also raided Spain's coasts and created trouble in the Caribbean, whereupon Philip II of Spain decided to invade England.

On 28 May 1588, 130 ships, most of them armed merchantmen, left Lisbon under the command of the Duke of Medina-Sidonia. On board were 8,000 sailors, 18,000 soldiers, and 2,500 guns. They intended to sail to Calais, meet the 30,000-strong Spanish Army of Flanders under the Duke of Parma, and escort it to England. The English, commanded by Lord Howard, totalled 200 ships, most of which were also armed merchantmen. In terms of firepower, the Spanish enjoyed a great advantage. After some preliminary skirmishes, during which the English used fireships, the Armada did in fact anchor opposite Calais, only to find that Dutch ships were making communications with Parma very difficult while also blocking the barges on which Parma's troops were supposed to embark.

Queen Elizabeth I of England, victor in the war against Spain.

The main action took place off the small port of Gravelines. The English ships were smaller and more manoeuvrable than the Spanish ones, enabling them to avoid the enemy's attempts at boarding. They also enjoyed the advantage of being windward, enabling them to open and end any action as they pleased. Five Spanish ships were lost and many damaged. Meanwhile, the inability of the Army of Flanders to rendezvous with the Armada had rendered the entire venture pointless. As the Armada tried to return to Spain by sailing around Scotland, first a major navigation error and then storms decimated it. In the end just sixty-seven ships and under 10,000 men, many of them desperately ill, made it home.

The defeat of the Armada did not end the war, which lasted until 1604. It did, however, mark a critical step on the road to Britain's command of the sea, which, with various ups and downs, was to last until 1919.

46

Outbreak of the Thirty Years War

1618

This was not the first religious war between Catholics and Protestants in Europe, having been preceded by the Schmalkaldic War (1546–47), the French Huguenot Wars (1562–98), and the Dutch Revolt against Spain (1568–1648). It was, however, the largest, most ferocious, and most deadly.

The war started in May 1618 when the Protestant estates of Bohemia revolted against the Catholic Emperor Ferdinand II. Had the revolt remained localised, it would have been suppressed fairly quickly. As, in fact, it almost was in 1620, when the Habsburgs and their allies won the Battle of the White Mountain. Instead it kept expanding. First the Hungarians and then the Ottomans were drawn in (though the latter did not stay in for long). Then came the Spaniards, then the Danes, then the Swedes, and finally the French. All sought to save their co-religionists, enforce their own religious creed, and grab as much territory as they could in Germany and the surrounding countries – with some more successful than others.

Caught in the maelstrom, many petty states, cities, and more or less independent robber barons also set up militias and joined what developed into a wild free for all. For three decades armies and militias chased each other all over central Europe, robbing, burning, raping, and killing on a scale unequalled until the twentieth century. By the time the Treaty of Westphalia ended the hostilities, the population of Germany had been reduced by approximately one-third.

Fought mainly by mercenary, often ill-disciplined, armies, the war saw many innovations. Chief among them were the demise of the arquebus and its replacement by the heavier musket; the introduction, by the Dutch, of drill; the appearance, in the form of the Swedish 'leather guns', of artillery sufficiently light to be moved not just to the battlefield but during the fighting; and the re-invention, also by the Swedes, of cavalry armed with edged weapons rather than with handguns. As a result, the Dutch and Swedish armies in particular became Europe's military academies.

The war failed to resolve the conflict between Catholics and Protestants. However, once it had ended the role of religion in international affairs started to decline. The greatest victor was France, which soon became the leading power on the continent. The greatest loser was Germany, which had been fragmented into hundreds of petty states with hardly the shadow of the Old Holy Roman Empire left to protect it.

47

Beijing Falls to the Qin of Manchuria

1644

In April 1644 an army of rebellious peasants under Li Zicheng captured the Chinese capital. Thereupon the Ming emperor, feeling he had lost the 'Mandate of Heaven', killed himself, thus bringing his dynasty to an end. As Li Zicheng and Ming loyalists fought each other the Qin, under Prince Dorgon, used the opportunity to invade China from the north. Defeating the Chinese in the critical Battle of Shanhai Pass, they opened the road into north-eastern China; early in June they entered Beijing.

But Beijing is not China. Many more campaigns were needed to subdue the rest of the country, especially the provinces Shaanxi (where Li Zicheng had retreated) and Sichuan. May 1645 found Dorgon in Jiangsu whose capital, Yangzhou, he captured. That done, he ordered the entire population to be massacred. Early in 1659 Qin troops, having overrun Guizhou and Yunnan, were able to force the new head of the Ming forces, known as the Yongli Emperor, to flee into nearby Burma. As had often been the case in the past, none of these operations would have been possible had large numbers of Chinese, guessing (correctly, as it turned out) who the victor would be, not joined the Qin armies and provided them with technical expertise. The more time passed, the more important the Chinese element became.

China being as large as it is, the Qin wars against the remaining opposition only ended in 1681. Even then it was still necessary to occupy Taiwan, where a self-appointed Ming loyalist, Zheng Chenggong (known to the world by his Dutch name, Koxinga), had established an independent principality. That accomplished, in 1683 the Qin victory, achieved at the cost of hundreds of thousands if not millions of lives, was complete.

The wars decided China's fate until 1911. The scale on which they were waged was immense; but they also provided conclusive proof that, in terms of military organisation, fortification, artillery, and firearms, as well the drill and tactics associated with them, China was falling behind the West. The gap, far from diminishing, kept growing. It only started to close after 1945.

48

Culmination of the Military Revolution

c. 1660

Many historians have questioned whether there ever was such a thing as the military revolution; on balance, though, the concept seems sufficiently useful to be included here.

The principal elements of the 'revolution' were as follows:

The **Peace of Westphalia** marked the end of the old feudal order and the rise of the modern state. Abolishing feudal levies, urban militias, and mercenaries, states replaced them with standing armies made up of long-time volunteers. The outcome was a vast increase in the size of armies and their subjection to strict centralised, bureaucratic control.

The **decline of cavalry**. Medieval and early sixteenth-century knights had been armoured from top to toe. Now armour was progressively discarded, until only heavy cavalry continued to wear it in the form of breast- and back-plates. Light cavalry, of which there were several kinds, and infantry did without any armour at all.

The **rise of infantry and artillery**. Infantry now formed the dominant element in all armies. Artillery also became more prominent, leading to a great increase in the number of barrels per soldier. Improved metallurgy enabled thinner barrels, which in turn meant lighter, more mobile pieces drawn by smaller teams. Originally operated by experts for hire, after 1660 artillery was fully incorporated into the military organisation.

The **invention of the bayonet** allowed armies to discard their last remaining pikemen in favour of a single kind of infantry. Armed with flintlocks, that infantry discarded the deep phalanxes in which it had been arrayed and started fighting in long, increasingly thin, lines – hence the name 'linear warfare'.

The invention of uniforms. Pioneered by the French, uniforms served three purposes: they distinguished soldiers from civilians; friend from foe; and units from each other. Over time they also became the subject of intense competition among sovereigns, each of whom wanted to outdo the other in coming up with most extravagant designs.

By 1715, **sailing ships had replaced galleys**. Previously there had been little difference between merchantmen and warships; but by 1690 'men of war' had become a distinct type. Carrying their guns on the sides, these ships fought in line ahead instead of prow to prow as previously.

Summing up, perhaps the best way to gauge the military revolution is ask what happened to the forces that did not go through it. Short answer: not too long thereafter, they ceased to count.

49

Beginning of Louis XIV's Wars

In his memoirs Louis XIV wrote that, having ascended the throne, his first thought was to gain glory 'as befits a prince'. He started with Franche-Comté and the Spanish Netherlands which, claiming his wife's inheritance, he invaded in 1667. This caused Spain, England, the Netherlands, and Sweden to unite against him. The war ended in the Treaty of Aix-la-Chapelle (1668), which gained Louis a number of fortresses in the southern Netherlands.

In 1672 Louis invaded the Netherlands proper. This time he had England on his side, whereas opposing him were the Netherlands, the Empire, Spain, and Brandenburg. At one point it was only by breaching the dykes that Holland was saved. The war, which ended in 1678 with the Treaty of Nijmegen, gained Louis France-Comté as well as additional land in the southern Netherlands.

In 1688 Louis, claiming to defend the rights of his sister-in-law, invaded the Palatinate. This time he was opposed by England and the Netherlands, now united under single rule, as well as the Empire, Spain, and Savoy. The war was fought in the Spanish Netherlands, southern Germany, and northern Italy. When it ended in 1697, Louis gained Alsace from the Empire.

Finally, in 1701 Louis' attempt to settle the Spanish Crown on his grandson, the Duke of Anjou, led to the War of the Spanish

Succession. Opposing Louis were England, the Netherlands, the Empire, and Savoy. Spain was divided between the two sides. The war ended in 1714 with the Treaty of Rastatt. The Austrians got most of Spain's European possessions; but Anjou received Spain, including its extra-European Empire. England (known, after 1707, as Great Britain) captured Gibraltar.

All these wars were waged both on land and at sea. The third and the fourth also extended to the European colonies in Asia and the Caribbean. Involving some 600,000 troops on the French side alone, the War of the Austrian Succession in particular was the largest fought in Europe since antiquity. As such, it foreshadowed the Great Power struggles to come.

All this earned Louis the nickname '*le roi de guerre*'. The wars saw some great commanders in action: the Frenchmen Condé, Turenne and Vauban; the imperial Prince Eugene of Savoy; and the Englishman Marlborough. Between them they accomplished the military revolution. Operationally, though, all but the last one were rather pettifogging, undertaking much manoeuvring and numerous sieges but few decisive battles.

50

Outbreak of the Great Northern War

Sweden's great warrior king, Gustavus Adolphus (r. 1611–32), and his successors had used the Thirty Years War to build an empire south of the Baltic. Now Denmark and Norway, Poland and Russia, the latter under Peter the Great, formed an alliance to partition it. But the coalition had not reckoned with Sweden's 18-year-old king, Charles XII, who turned out to be a military genius. First, forming an alliance with the Dutch, he launched a lightning naval attack on Copenhagen and forced Denmark out of the war. Next, turning around, in 1706 he defeated August the Strong, King of Poland, at the battles Kliszów and Fraustadt.

In 1709 Charles invaded Russia. But Peter refused to give battle, withdrawing into the depths of his country while leaving scorched earth behind. The two sides finally met at Poltava on the Vorskla River. Seeing that sheer élan had helped them win previous battles, the Swedes, though weakened by hunger and disease and greatly outnumbered, tried to storm the Russians' fortified camp. The Russian Army had recently been reformed on the Western model. It now consisted of long-term conscripts with professional officers, drawn from the nobility and serving for life, to command them. Forming lines abreast, four ranks deep, they fired volley after volley into the enemy. The Swedish attempt failed, and Peter's forces counter-attacked. Charles XII, wounded in the foot, with his remaining troops, was forced to escape across the Ukraine into Ottoman-held territory to the south.

With Charles out of the picture, the anti-Swedish alliance, reinforced by Hanover and Prussia, was restored. The last Swedish possession south of the Baltic, Riga, was lost in 1710. Returning home in 1714, Charles found that his country's outnumbered forces had been unable to save Finland from the Russians. His attempt to restore the situation by invading Norway failed, and he himself was killed at Fredriksten in 1718.

The war finally ended in 1721, but not before a Russian fleet, newly created by Peter the Great, had raided Stockholm itself. When peace finally came Sweden lost all the lands south of the Baltic. Its place as the dominant power in that region was taken by Russia, which now for the first time became an active player in the affairs of Western Europe.

51

Outbreak of the War of the Austrian Succession

1740

The War of the Austrian Succession began when Frederick II of Prussia tried to grab Silesia from Austria. It quickly developed into a pan-European free for all focusing around the greatest powers of the time: Austria and France. Other theatres where it was fought included the southern Netherlands, Germany, Bohemia, northern Italy, North America, and India. Naval actions took place as far afield as the West Indies, the Mediterranean, Northern Waters, and the Indian Ocean

By this time the military of all the major belligerents had been fully professionalised. Officers were aristocrats and gentlemen; one subject taught in every one of the newly established military academies was dancing. The troops were low-class commoners drawn mostly from the countryside – 'The scum of the earth, enlisted for drink,' as the British commander Wellington later put it. Pikes had disappeared, making Clausewitz take 1740 as the beginning of 'modern' war. Sieges and murderous battles – the latter fought at close range between long lines of musket-carrying infantry that was flanked and supported by cavalry and artillery – punctuated endless complicated manoeuvres. Designed to lever the opponent out of his position with the objective of either preparing for a decisive battle or achieving victory without having to fight one, those manoeuvres seldom succeeded in doing either. More or less massive naval battles were fought by British, French, and Spanish warships sailing in line ahead and cannonading each other, sometimes thousands of miles from home.

Perhaps the most important battle of the war was that of Fontenoy in May 1745. The French commander, Maurice Marshal de France, with 52,000 men, defeated an Anglo-Dutch-Hanoverian army of similar size, leading to the capture of much of the southern Netherlands. The battle was followed, a month later, by that of Hohenfriedberg in Silesia. On this occasion Prussian troops, though outnumbered, decisively defeated the Austrians and Saxons, earning Frederick the epithet 'the Great'. When peace came in 1748, Prussia gained Silesia, whereas the British and French exchanged some territories in both North America and India.

The war marked the beginning of Prussia's rise to Great Power status. It also saw important developments in the law of war, such as in treating prisoners, the wounded, etc. Codified by the great lawyer Emmerich Vattel, these developments became the basis of 'civilised' warfare as practised, more or less, until 1939.

52

Outbreak of the Seven Years War

1756

Again, the Seven Years War started with an attack by Prussia's Frederick II on Austria, though this time it was pre-emptive. Again, it quickly escalated until all of Europe's main powers were involved. This time, however, France and Austria were allies – something that had not happened for centuries and which, with one brief interruption (1812), was not to happen again.

In 1756 Frederick overran Saxony. In 1757 he tried to capture Prague but failed; that year also saw the most famous battles of the war, Rossbach and Leuthen, in which his outnumbered, but well-trained and firmly disciplined, troops beat the French and the Austrians respectively. Simultaneously he came under attack by Russia whose troops at one point occupied Berlin. Ferociously defending himself by attacking now on one front, now on another, Frederick was barely able to hold out. Some battles he won, others lost. Others still ended in draws but brought losses which Prussia, the smallest of the Great Powers, could ill afford. Had not Elizabeth of Russia died in 1762 and been replaced by his admirer Peter III, Frederick and his kingdom would have been utterly crushed.

The war was also waged in north-western Germany, where the Hanoverian Army, financed by Frederick's ally Britain, held the French at bay. Perhaps more important for the future of

the world were the struggles in North America and India. In both theatres the British prevailed over the French. The war was also waged in South America, where Britain's Portuguese allies fought the Spaniards, as well as in the Caribbean and West Africa. There, too, Britain took over some important French possessions.

As far as the available communications allowed, all these fronts were coordinated from the respective capitals; thus it would hardly be an exaggeration to say that the Seven Years War was the first truly global war. Indigenous levies also played a role, especially in North America and India. However, in both theatres the warriors' bravery was of little avail in frontal clashes with the Europeans' superior equipment and organisation.

The war made Britain, under Prime Minister Pitt, the world's strongest naval power. This position it retained until 1919. On land, all eyes were on the Prussian Army and the famous 'oblique order' in which it fought and triumphed. This was to cost Prussia dear: in 1806 its army, having sat on its laurels for forty years, was smashed by Napoleon.

53 Battle of Plassey

1757

The background to the Battle of Plassey was formed by the attack of the 23-year-old new Nawab of Bengal, Siraj ud-Daulah, on the British fort and factory of Calcutta. With 50,000 men, including infantry, cavalry, and some artillery, he had little difficulty overcoming the resistance of some 500 troops of the English East Indian Company. Famously, 146 prisoners were put into the 'Black Hole of Calcutta'. Only twenty-three of them emerged alive.

Counter-attacking, in June the British met their opponents at Plassey, north of Calcutta. The forces on both sides were as ill matched as any in history. The Nawab had no fewer than 50,000 men, armed with a mixture of edged weapons and matchlocks. To them the British commander, Robert Clive, could only oppose 600 Europeans and 2,100 sepoys (natives). In terms of artillery pieces (the Bengali ones were served by French personnel), the Nawab outnumbered Clive by no less than ninety-four to eight.

Starting at 8 a.m., for three hours the two sides fired at each other with little effect. On the Bengali side this was because heavy rain soaked their powder, whereas the British had taken the precaution of covering theirs with tarpaulins. Shortly after noon the Bengalis launched an attack on the British. It was, however, repulsed with loss. Thereupon Clive, counter-attacking,

Siraj ud-Daulah, the Rajah whose defeat at Plassey marked the beginning of British domination in India.

drove back the French artillery and occupied the position from which it had been firing. Holding that position, he was able not only to beat off several counter-attacks but to bombard the Nawab's camp. By 5 p.m. his troops were in possession of the camp while the Nawab's army was melting away. 'Melting away' is the right term: Clive himself estimated that the Bengalis had lost no more than 500 men, including several key commanders. His own losses, both European and native, amounted to about 100. Not long thereafter Siraj was murdered by one of his own men.

The battle brought a large part of north-eastern India under British control for the first time. It was followed by the naval encounter at Coromandel, fought in April 1758 south of Pondicherry. Together these two engagements ensured that India should become British, not French. If the figures are to be believed, in the whole of history it is hard to find another example when such a small force defeated such a large one.

54

Beginning of the Wars of Catherine the Great

1769

The War of the Austrian Succession and the Seven Years War, during which the principal European powers had fought each other, gave the Ottomans a long respite from their most dangerous enemies. It ended in September 1769, when the Tsaritsa, Catherine the Great, sent her armies south to combat them. First they captured the fortress of Khotyn, now in the Ukraine's south-western corner. This victory caused Voltaire, who fancied himself Catherine's friend, to rhapsodise about 'the Minerva of the North' who was going to 'avenge Greece by chasing out the [Turkish] reprobates'.

On 7 July 1770, on the river Larga, a tributary of the Prut now in Moldova, 38,000 Russians under Field Marshal Rumyantsev defeated an Ottoman–Tartar coalition twice their number. With that, the remnants of Tartar independence came to an end. Three weeks later, on 1 August 1770, Rumyantsev beat another Ottoman force at Kagul in southern Bessarabia. Both times the Russians assaulted their enemies, causing many casualties. This victory opened the way to Bucharest, which they captured. Meanwhile, a Russian fleet had sailed through the Dardanelles. Encountering an Ottoman fleet nearly twice its own size not far from Cesma, on the west Anatolian coast, the Russians blew their opponents out of the water.

Major hostilities having ended, Catherine turned her attention to Poland, which she divided with Prussia and Austria. In 1796,

shortly before her death, she went to war again, this time with Persia over Georgia. At issue were the lands east of the Black Sea, a region that had been a Russian protectorate since 1763. The scale of hostilities was considerably smaller: only 13,000 Russians took part. Even so they were able to take the major fortress of Derbent, after which the cities of Baku, Shemakha, and Ganja fell almost without resistance. By the end of the year all Azerbaijan had been overrun, which meant that the Russians were now positioned to invade Persia proper.

The wars proved, if proof were needed, that European-style forces no longer had a worthwhile opponent anywhere on earth. Previously the government at St Petersburg had only owned a toehold on the Black Sea. Now it had completed the occupation of the Ukraine and more or less turned that sea into a Russian lake. The wars formed a critical step in the process that was to turn Russia into a Great Power not only on the Baltic and in the Far East, but in the south as well.

55

First Shots in the War of the American Revolution

Once the British had taken Canada from the French in 1763, friction between them and their American colonies developed almost immediately, finally resulting in open hostilities. The first battles – in reality, skirmishes that only claimed 122 dead on both sides combined – were fought near Boston. Using guerrilla tactics, the colonists forced the greatly outnumbered British regulars to evacuate the city.

Greatly overestimating their own success, the Americans tried to take Québec, but failed. Thereupon the Colonies, now united under the Continental Congress in Philadelphia, established the Continental Army, appointing George Washington to command it. Washington, though, was outmanoeuvred by the British commander, Sir William Howe, who captured New York and held it until the end of the war.

Crossing the Delaware to the south, Washington, having fought and won the Battle of Trenton, created a base in New Jersey. Meanwhile the British, having received reinforcements, mounted an all-out effort to suppress the rebellion. One prong under John Burgoyne, consisting of some 7,000 men, advanced from Canada by way of the Hudson Valley, only to be trapped at Saratoga by a somewhat larger American force and compelled to surrender. The other, under Howe himself, tried to capture Philadelphia but failed.

At this point France, seeking revenge for its defeat in the Seven Years War, allied itself with the Colonies, bringing Spain

George Washington.

with it. This did not prevent the British, now commanded by Charles Cornwallis, from focusing their efforts on the south and taking Savanna and Charleston. From there they marched north into Virginia. On 19 October 1781 the two sides met at Yorktown. As the French fleet had previously defeated the British one at Chesapeake Bay, the British only had 7,000 men to face a combined Franco-American force three times as large. They were defeated and compelled to surrender, bringing about the fall of the British Cabinet and moving Britain towards eventual peace.

The war started with an uprising by American militiamen ('Minutemen') against Britain's regulars. Later, from his base in New Jersey, Washington strove mightily to turn his own Continentals into a regular, professional force modelled on the British one. However, he never quite made it. Down to the end, militias continued to play an important role both in the Carolinas and in the west, where the British were assisted by Indian irregulars.

56

Outbreak of the French Revolutionary Wars

Three years after the beginning of the Revolution, King Louis XVI was compelled to declare war on Prussia and Austria. Along with Spain, the latter invaded France, resulting in a half-hearted endeavour that was stopped by the 'cannonade' of Valmy in September. Of this clash Goethe, an eyewitness, said that it opened a new epoch in human history, there and then.

Instituting general mobilisation (the famous *levée en masse*) – the first time this had been done in Europe for centuries – and replacing the old aristocratic officers with bourgeois ones, the French were able to raise enormous armies. They fought back ferociously and invaded their neighbours in turn. Most of the action took place in the southern (Austrian) Netherlands and southern Germany. Among the principal turning points were the battles of Jemappes, in Belgium, in November 1792, when the French defeated the Austrians; that of Fleurus, also in Belgium, in June 1794, which ended in another huge victory of the French over the Austrians; and of the Black Mountain in Catalonia in November of the same year, where the French defeated a combined Spanish–Portuguese force. These wars ended with the Peace of Basel (1795), which left the French in possession of parts of the southern Netherlands as well as the Rhineland.

The war with Austria continued. In 1796 the French Army of Italy, commanded by a 26-year-old general by the name of Napoleon Bonaparte, crossed the Alps into the Po Valley. Here a series of lightning operations, fought on internal lines as the French beat their opponents in detail, led to the fall first of Milan, then of Rome, and finally of the whole of Italy. Lasting until 1797, this campaign cost the Austrians 150,000 men in prisoners alone.

In 1798 Napoleon went to Egypt, enabling Austria to reassert itself. Returning home in 1799, he mounted a coup, made himself first consul, and resumed hostilities. Early in 1800 he formed a so-called Armée de Réserve at Dijon, took it across the Alps in midwinter, and attacked the Austrians, busily besieging Genoa, in the rear. This series of war ended with the great French victory at Marengo and brought the whole of Italy under French control. The French triumphs culminated at Hohenlinden, in Bavaria, in December, when General Moreau crushed the Austrians. This left Britain, which had entered the wars in 1798, isolated. In 1801 general peace was restored by the Treaty of Amiens.

57

Outbreak of the Napoleonic Wars

<u>1803</u>

By the time Britain decided to go to war against France again, Napoleon had become sole ruler of that country. Not only was he to show himself to be one of the greatest commanders of all times, but he had at his disposal what was probably the most powerful army in history until that time.

Originally Napoleon intended to invade Britain. However, the power of the Royal Navy, combined with losses due to stormy weather at sea, caused him to change his mind. He was saved from his predicament by Austria, which declared war on him. Turning his army around, he marched into Germany, defeated the Austrians at Ulm, and entered Vienna. From there he went on to Austerlitz, in Moravia. On 2 December 1805 he crushed the combined armies of Austria and Russia. Unfortunately for him, six weeks earlier the British under Nelson had destroyed his fleet at Trafalgar, ending any hope of victory on that front. It led him to declare a blockade of the British Isles, known as the Continental System.

In September 1806 Prussia declared war on France. Marching into northern Germany, Napoleon crushed the Prussians at Jena and occupied Berlin. Next he went on to fight the Russians in Poland and defeated them, albeit at heavy cost, in the battles of Eylau and Friedland in 1807. The next year found him in Iberia, where he occupied Spain and most of Portugal, though he

Admiral Nelson.

failed to take Lisbon and found his forces engaged in a long and vicious war against a British army as well as Spanish guerrillas. In 1809 the Austrians, invading Napoleon's ally Bavaria, took him by surprise. He was, however, able to stop them at Eckmühl and Wagram, once again occupying Vienna.

In June 1812, now in command of no fewer than 600,000 troops gathered from many European nations, Napoleon invaded Russia which, like Spain before it, had refused to cooperate in the Continental System. He defeated the Tsar's army at Borodino and occupied Moscow. However, he was unable to dictate peace; retreating west, he lost most of his army to General Winter (as it was called) and pursuing Cossacks. In October 1813 he faced another coalition, this time of Russians, Prussians, Austrians, and Swedes, at Leipzig, where 280,000 allies crushed his 180,000 men. Retreating into France, in early 1814 he was still able to conduct some brilliant manoeuvres before overwhelming enemy forces defeated him and forced him to abdicate in April 1814.

58

Outbreak of the Wars of Latin American Independence

1808

What made these wars possible were Napoleon's occupation of Spain and the subsequent collapse of Spanish government in Latin America. As a result, juntas (committees) made up of Creoles (white Spaniards born in the colonies) were set up in many key Latin American cities. In 1810–12 several of them declared their independence from Spain.

The wars' early years were characterised by guerrilla action and numerous small skirmishes between the opposing sides. Small they had to be, for Madrid never had more than 10,000 men to dominate a huge continent. It is true, however, that both sides were assisted by native levies ten times more numerous than their own troops.

The first large-scale clashes took place in Mexico in 1810. In September 30,000 rebels under Miguel Hidalgo y Costilla defeated a Spanish force at Guanajuato, in central Mexico. From there they marched on Mexico City. However, the loyalists, with just 1,000 men, 400 horsemen, and 2 cannon, were able to hold out. At Coahuila in 1811 they defeated Hidalgo, who was captured and executed. Thereupon guerrilla warfare resumed. Only in 1821 was the Spanish Colonel Agustín de Iturbide, turning rebel and exploiting political disorder in Madrid, finally able to defeat his former colleagues at Oaxaca.

Invading Venezuela from New Granada in 1812–13, the rebel leader Símon Bolívar won several victories over the loyalist

A mounted warrior during the Wars of Latin American Liberation.

forces but suffered as many defeats in turn. Only in 1819, at Carabobo, did his 8,000 or so troops finally overcome a slightly smaller Spanish one, thus securing the country's independence. Meanwhile, to the south, another army was formed under José de San Martín. Starting in 1817, he crossed the Andes from Argentina, joined with the Chilean general Bernardo O'Higgins, and fought his way up north all the way into Peru.

By 1822 the independence of Mexico and Spanish South America was assured, though arriving at a political settlement took longer. Relatively small as the forces on both sides were, the prolonged struggle, consisting partly of guerrilla warfare and partly of civil war, was horrifically bloody. The total number of dead is said to have been about 600,000. By contrast, Brazilian independence from Portugal was achieved practically without bloodshed: when about 10,000 armed people surrounded the commander of the Portuguese garrison at Monte Castelo, Rio de Janeiro, in January 1822, he surrendered. In return, he and his men were allowed to leave for Portugal.

59

War of 1812

The War of 1812 originated in friction between the US and Britain over the latter's impressment of American sailors to serve in its navy as well as its support for Native American tribes, which were at loggerheads with the US. It was fought in three separate, widely dispersed theatres. One was the Atlantic, where both sides' warships and privateers attacked each other's merchant vessels. The British also blockaded the American coast and, late in the war, used the rivers to launch large-scale raids inland. The second was the US–Canadian frontier, which saw battles both on land and on the Great Lakes. The third was the south-east and America's Gulf coast.

At the time US President John Adams declared war, Britain was fully engaged with Napoleon, leaving few forces to spare for North America. This fact, as well as the Native Americans' own weakness, explains why the latter were quickly defeated and any attempt to set up a British-sponsored Native American Confederacy in the west was frustrated. American vessels on Lake Erie also defeated British ones, leading to an invasion of western Canada. However, an American attempt to capture Montreal in the autumn of 1813 failed. Next, the British drove their enemies back to Fort Erie, which they besieged for several months.

Following Napoleon's first abdication in April 1814, the British brought up reinforcements. Making full use of their

'The Star-Spangled Banner' – written in the midst of the war of 1812.

unrivalled naval power, they occupied eastern Maine and raided Washington, burning the White House. However, their attempts to do the same at Baltimore (during which 'The Star-Spangled Banner' was written) and New York failed. Meanwhile negotiations were under way at Ghent, Belgium. A peace treaty had already been signed at Ghent when American forces under future president Andrew Jackson defeated the British at New Orleans in January 1815.

Whereas, at Leipzig, both sides together deployed almost half a million men, at New Orleans the Americans had 5,000 and the British 11,000. The remaining engagements in the war, which took place in a huge and sparsely populated country, were much smaller still. The war ended any idea of an independent Native American Confederacy in the west. Though the border between the US and Canada remained unchanged, it was only after 1865 that it was formally extended to the Pacific coast. Above all, the war put a final seal on the existence of the US as an independent country.

60

Waterloo and the End of the Napoleonic Wars

1815

Thanks to mass mobilisation, Napoleon had waged war on a scale never before achieved. A proper command system, plus the division of the army into corps each of which was capable of limited independent action, permitted him to advance on a broad front. This in turn enabled him to bypass most fortresses, thereby avoiding prolonged and costly siege warfare that had frustrated so many of his predecessors. Exercising his strategic genius to the full, time and again he caught his opponents at a disadvantage and crushed them. As he himself recognised in 1813, though, '*ces animaux ont apprenu quelque chose*' – 'These animals [i.e. his enemies] have learnt something'.

Returning from Elbe in March 1815, Napoleon found the whole of Europe united against him. By quickly taking the offensive, though, he ensured that only the Prussians, the British, and the Dutch would be present to oppose him in the field. On 15 June he invaded Belgium with 130,000 men divided into six corps. He crossed the Sambre at Charleroi and, having defeated the Prussians under Blücher in the Battle of Ligny, forced them to retreat north-east. Meanwhile Marshal Ney, at Quatre Bras on Napoleon's left, held off the British commander, Wellington. Both these battles were French victories. But they did not suffice to drive the allies back far enough to enable Napoleon to use his favourite strategy of beating his enemies in detail.

Napoleon Bonaparte – the man who invented strategy.

The main clash between the two sides took place at Waterloo on the 18th. The French had 73,000 men present, the British (with various small allies) 68,000, and the Prussians 50,000. The battle opened in the morning with a series of ferocious French frontal attacks on the British lines. Meanwhile Napoleon had sent his cavalry under Grouchy to outflank the Prussians on the right. Grouchy did in fact defeat the Prussians at Wavre, but was unable to stop them from marching towards the sound of the guns at Waterloo. Losing communications with Napoleon, he was not present when and where the main clash took place. The battle was decided during the afternoon when the Prussians came marching from the north-east, reinforcing the British and taking the French in the right flank. A last desperate attack by Napoleon's Guard Corps failed. Three days later, in Paris, Napoleon abdicated – and the series of war that had started in 1792 finally ended.

Part IV

INDUSTRIAL WAR

1815–1945 CE

61

Beginning of the French Conquest of Algeria

<u>1830</u>

The war between France and Algeria originated in some commercial disputes between France and the Ottoman governor of Algiers, Hussein Dey. Another factor was Algerian piracy in the Mediterranean. The outcome was a massive French invasion of the country, which the Ottoman commanders, in spite of having at their disposal more troops (43,000 to 34,000), were unable to resist. In July 1830, after a three-week campaign, the French, under General de Bourmont, entered Algiers. Four years later the French formally annexed Algeria, thus bringing an estimated population of 2 million under their control.

This political act did not put an end to the war. Most of the fighting took place in the western part of the country where a local leader, Abd al-Qadir, succeeded in having himself recognised as Amir (commander) of the faithful. Only in 1836 did the French, now commanded by Marshal Bugeaud, succeed in defeating him at Sikkak. From this point on the struggle increasingly assumed the character of guerrilla warfare, conducted by raiders and saboteurs (on the Algerian side) and by flying columns (on the French). A key role was played by

In the 1830s the French started campaigning in Algeria, turning it into a colony.

watering points, which both sides tried to control. The struggle only ended, to the extent that it ever did, when the French succeeded in hemming in al-Qadir and his remaining men between themselves and Moroccan troops who cooperated with them. Forced to surrender, ultimately al-Qadir was allowed to settle in Damascus.

The war, in which the rules of 'civilised' warfare did not apply, was waged with great ferocity on both sides. Not for nothing did it witness, in 1831, the establishment of the Foreign Legion, to be known much later as the 'White SS'. Repeating the lesson of Napoleon's 1798 invasion of Egypt and Palestine, it showed to the world that Arab forces were no match for superior French (and Western) organisation and weapons. It also marked a critical step in the process by which the Europeans set out to divide the non-European world among themselves.

62

Publication of Clausewitz's *On War*

<u>1832</u>

In every field, there are plenty of good books. Not so when it comes to the theory of war. Sun Tzu's *Art of War* apart, there is just one: Carl von Clausewitz's *On War*.

Clausewitz, a Prussian, served as a staff officer and eventually made it to general. However, he never commanded large formations in war. From 1815 on he devoted himself mainly to study. Two questions dominate his work. First, what war is; and second, what it serves for.

Clausewitz's famous answer to the second question is that war is the continuation of politics by other means. It follows that, at the higher levels, war, instead of obeying its own logic, should be governed by politics. From Clausewitz's day to ours, applying that rule has proved easier said than done. Rulers and commanders-in-chief often interfere with each other; each also tends to accuse the other of failing to understand the other's métier.

The answer to the first question is that war is a duel written large. Its essence is action and reaction; a single blow does not war make. The best strategy is to be very strong, first in general and then at the decisive point. Offense and defence – Clausewitz considers the latter the stronger form of war – interact. An offensive that does not achieve its objectives fairly quickly will reach a culminating point and turn into a defence. The need to

Carl von Clausewitz, regarded by many as the greatest military theorist ever.

work with large numbers of men, often under difficult conditions and while trying to preserve secrecy, makes the conduct of war very difficult. This is the origin of what Clausewitz, again famously, calls 'friction'.

War, a social phenomenon, is a chameleon. Ever fluid, ever changing, it cannot be encapsulated by hard and fast rules. The most important factors that make for success are 1, mass; 2, morale; and 3, surprise. The latter, however, works better at the lower, tactical level than on the higher, strategic one.

For Clausewitz, war is governed by a 'remarkable trinity'. It is made up of the directing intellect; fighting power; and the fierce hatred that causes and inspires the struggle. The first is represented by the government, the second by the armed forces, the third by the civilian population. Except for a few pages devoted to 'The People in Arms', Clausewitz takes the distinction between these groups very much for granted. Today, however, it applies less often – which is why some regard the master's work as outdated.

63

Beginning of the Military-Technological Revolution

c. 1835

Technologically speaking, the eighteenth century was rather conservative. For example, the British musket, nicknamed 'Brown Bess', remained in service for a hundred years. The origins of the industrial revolution are usually traced back to the 1760s. However, field armies had to be mobile, with the result that they only began to feel the impact from about 1835 on. This helps explain why Clausewitz, for one, barely mentions military technology.

The first major innovations were railways and telegraphs. They revolutionised the speed at which armies could be mobilised, vastly increased strategic mobility, and enabled widely dispersed forces to communicate with each other and with headquarters. Next came the percussion cap, a small but important invention which greatly accelerated the speed of loading and allowed the troops to do so even when it was raining. This in turn opened the way to the introduction of rifled, breech-loading arms and cannon. By 1870 steel was being used to cast the latter, making possible larger charges, and therefore greater range, at reduced weight.

Between 1865 and 1880, first magazine rifles and then smokeless powder were introduced. In the 1890s they were followed by recoil mechanisms, making it unnecessary to re-sight the guns after each round. Machine guns, capable of firing 600 rounds a minute, also appeared. So, after 1900, did motor cars and a few prototype tanks. Radio, which rid armies of wires and revolutionised command and control at sea, was introduced at about the same time.

During the 1860s naval vessels started to be provided with steam engines. Early on wooden ships were covered with steel plating; from about 1870, though, vessels were made entirely of steel. One outcome was a vast increase in their size. Cannon, both naval and stationary (in coastal batteries), grew to monstrous dimensions. By 1914 the largest had 15in calibre and could fire a 1-ton shell to a distance of 30km. Fire controls were also revolutionised. Meanwhile, operating in the depths, submarines armed with torpedoes started challenging surface fleets for the first time.

Finally, the years after 1900 saw the first military use of 'flying machines', both lighter and heavier than air. The earliest models were used for reconnaissance both over land and at sea. Soon, however, they were armed and started fighting each other as well as influencing operations in both environments. Together, these inventions probably made the years from 1830 to 1914 the most transformative in the entire history of war.

64 Outbreak of the Opium Wars

1839

The first Opium War broke out as a result of Emperor Daoguang's attempt to stop the British from importing opium from India into China. As part of this attempt Daoguang's government confiscated an immense quantity of opium without compensation, suspended foreign trade, and had foreign traders confined to their quarters. In response the British tried to take Taiwan, but were thrown back by a spirited defence. Subsequently British warships sailed up the Pearl River and the Yangtze, where the troops they carried captured the cities of Canton and Shanghai respectively. They also captured the emperor's treasure barges – an immense loss to China. The war ended in 1842 with the Treaty of Nanjing, which restored trade and obliged China to pay reparations and cede Hong Kong.

In 1856 further disputes over trade, during which the Chinese government accused the Europeans of engaging in piracy, led to the outbreak of the Second Opium War. This time France and the US joined Britain. In 1858, 6,000 allied troops bombarded Canton, a city with over a million inhabitants, and captured it. In the next year they overcame the Taku Forts, sailed up the Hai River, and marched on Beijing. In October, having defeated attempts by China's old-fashioned cavalry to stop them, they entered the city and plundered it, whereupon the Treaty of Tianjin ended the war by legalising the opium trade, awarding compensation to England and France, and granting foreign countries a permanent diplomatic presence in China. In addition, the Russians blackmailed China into ceding the non-freezing territories on the Pacific where they later built the port of Vladivostok.

The most remarkable feature of the wars is that they were waged by the Europeans (and the Americans) many thousands of miles away from their centres of power. Consequently they could never deploy more than a few thousand troops at any one time and place. Yet these small forces proved that pre-industrial armed armies and navies, however large and however brave, were hopelessly outclassed by modern ships (a few of them steam-operated), modern cannon, and modern rifles. Also that China, as the world's last major non-European power, was helpless against Europe's depredations. Thus the wars marked the beginning of China's so-called 'century of humiliation', which only ended when Mao Zedong and the communists took over the country in 1949.

65

Outbreak of the Mexican–American War

<u>1846</u>

The background to this war was formed by the 1845 American annexation of Texas, which the Mexican government could not and did not accept. An American attempt to buy New Mexico and California for $30 million was rebuffed. Thereupon US President James Polk opened hostilities, sending General Zachary Taylor to occupy the disputed area between the Nueces and the Rio Grande.

The first armed clashes took place in April when Mexican troops crossed the Rio Grande and attacked Taylor, injuring sixteen of his men. Congress having duly declared war, the US offensive developed along three main axes. First, Taylor advanced south from the Rio Grande into the heart of Mexico, captured the city of Monterrey, and defeated General Santa Anna at Buena Vista. Second, Colonel Stephen Kearney invaded New Mexico and California, whose main population centres he occupied against very little resistance.

However, neither advance even came close to securing final victory. To escape his critics, who accused him of aggression, Polk appointed General Winfield Scott to lead a naval expedition to Veracruz. Having captured that city, Scott marched inland on Mexico City and captured it as well. That accomplished, in September 1847 the military phase of the conflict came to an end. Later, under the Treaty of Guadalupe, the US paid Mexico

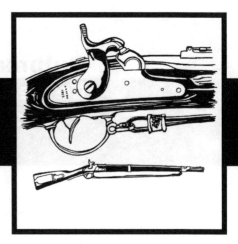

The Mexican War (1746–48) was one of the last to be fought with flintlocks.

$5 million for almost all the territory now forming the states of New Mexico, Utah, Nevada, Arizona, California, Texas, and western Colorado.

On both sides, the war was fought by tiny regular forces supported by a much larger number of short-time, often undisciplined and rowdy, volunteers. In the case of the US, the latter outnumbered the former by more than ten to one; the corresponding Mexican figures are impossible to come by, but must have been as skewed. Another outstanding characteristic of the conflict was the enormous spaces, which in turn made for an exceptionally low ratio of troops per square mile of land. Perhaps it would be true to say that seldom in history did so few men fight for such an enormous territory, comprising as it did no fewer than 2.1 million square kilometres.

Technologically speaking, the war was one of the very last to be fought with flintlocks little changed since pre-Napoleonic times. However, the introduction on the US side of the so-called Mississippi rifle, which used percussion caps, marked the beginning of the transition towards more modern weaponry.

66 Outbreak of the Crimean War

1853

One authority called it 'the war that refused to boil', a mere footnote to the on-going struggle of the Great Powers, all but one of which were, by this time, European. That may be true; but the war did show what, in the industrial age, would happen to any of those powers that fell behind the rest, militarily, technologically, and economically.

The prelude to the war was formed by a Russian invasion of the Ottoman-ruled principalities forming modern Romania. At the same time the Russian fleet destroyed the Ottoman one at Sinope, off the north Anatolian coast. Thereupon Austria, Britain and France joined forces in an attempt to force the Russians to retreat – a goal they finally achieved during the summer of 1854. Next, in September of the same year, a combined Anglo-French force set sail from Varna to the Crimea, which the successors of Catherine the Great had made into the main Russian naval base in the Black Sea. The landings on the peninsula were successfully carried out. However, the Russians, exploiting some allied errors, retreated to the city of Sevastopol, which resisted all efforts to capture it.

As the struggle in the Crimea was reduced to a war of attrition, minor hostilities also took place in other theatres. Notable among them were the Kerch Peninsula (where the allies also landed), the Caucasus (where the Russians made some gains at the expense of the Ottomans), the Baltic (where Anglo-French fleets did much as they pleased) and the White Sea (where they tried to take Archangelsk but failed). The main action, though, centred on Sevastopol. The city's capture, which took place in 1855 after a siege that had lasted a full year, convinced the Russians that they had no choice but to admit defeat and accept unfavourable terms.

On both sides, but especially the Russian and British ones, the conduct of the war was characterised by gross administrative and logistical mismanagement. On both sides, the outcome was vast numbers of casualties due to illness and neglect. In the West, both the mismanagement and the casualties were brought to the public's attention by means of the telegraph, which served the new mass-circulation newspapers of the time. The Russians, on their part, were shocked to discover their own backwardness, which among other things led to the liberation of the serfs in 1861.

67

Franco-Austrian War

1859

The Italian (in truth, north Italian) struggle of independence from Austria started during the 1830s. 1848 saw some uprisings as well as a Sardinian attempt to intervene, but they were defeated. Only in 1859 did the Italians, led by Sardinia, find a powerful sponsor in the form of France under Louis-Napoléon.

The total number of troops on each side was about 240,000; however, the Austrians had more artillery and more cavalry. The war started when the Austrian commander, Count Gyulay, tried to march on the Sardinian capital of Turin. However, his opponents flooded the fields through which he had to pass; this, as well as his own caution, prevented him from capturing it. Retreating, the Austrians abandoned Milan, whereupon Emperor Franz Joseph fired Gyulay and assumed command in person. The two sides, each commanded by its own emperor, fought several engagements in which the French were generally successful. The climax came at Solferino, near the River Ticino, on 24 June. On this occasion the French broke through the Austrian centre, forcing a general retreat. Reporting the outcome to his wife, the Empress Eugénie, Napoléon telegraphed, '*grande battaile, grande victoire.*'

In April 1860, Giuseppe Garibaldi and his redshirts took advantage of Austria's defeat to help found the modern Italian state.

While casualties on both sides were heavy, the battle all but ended the hostilities. The subsequent Treaty of Villafranca gave Milan to Sardinia. In return, France got Nice and Savoy, as well as a daughter of the King of Sardinia for Napoléon's cousin to marry. But that did not end the matter. First, violating the Treaty, the Sardinians occupied the small principalities of central Italy. Second, in April 1860, Giuseppe Garibaldi, an Italian rebel and adventurer with a long record of colourful exploits behind him, left Genoa at the head of 1,000 volunteers. Protected by French and British warships, he landed in Sicily. There he and his men were joined by many locals and drove the Bourbon Army in front of them until they entered the capital of Naples. Together with Sardinian troops, coming from the north, for the first time in many centuries they turned Italy from a geographical expression into a state.

68

Outbreak of the American Civil War

1861

The background to the war was formed by the need to keep the Union intact against attempts by the southern states, motivated by disputes over slavery and trade, to secede. Immediately following Lincoln becoming president, the first shots were fired by the Confederates at Fort Sumter in April 1861.

The Union's population at the time stood at 18.5 million, and that of the Confederacy at 9 million (including 3.5 million slaves). The Union was industrialised and capable of producing every kind of military equipment; the Confederacy was rural and had to rely on improvisation and imported arms. But the Confederacy enjoyed the advantage of being on the defensive and operating on internal lines. These facts dictated the shape of the war which was fought in four widely different theatres.

First, advancing along the eastern coast, the Federals tried to march on the Confederate capital at Richmond, but failed. Instead, they found themselves fighting off two Confederate invasions of Pennsylvania (in 1862 and 1863). Second, a series of complicated operations along the Mississippi River enabled the Union forces, moving from north to south, first to make Kentucky abandon its neutrality and then to invade Tennessee, from where they eventually continued into Georgia. Third, after the Union Navy captured New Orleans in 1862, Union forces advanced north along the Mississippi, capturing Vicksburg in July 1863 and cutting the Confederacy in half. The fourth theatre consisted of the Atlantic Ocean and the Gulf, where Union

A Gatling gun, one of the first machine guns to see action.

naval forces imposed and maintained an increasingly effective blockade of the Confederacy.

The end arrived in April 1865 after Union General Sherman, coming from the west, had captured Atlanta and advanced to the sea, whereas General Grant, coming from the north after a long campaign of attrition, captured Petersburg and Richmond. Outnumbered and starving, the last Confederate army under General Lee surrendered.

Waged on a massive scale, the war saw the use of many new devices. Including Minié rifles with expanding balls, repeating (magazine) rifles, Gatling guns, and balloons. Some campaigns, especially the siege of Petersburg, led to prolonged trench warfare. The war also witnessed experimental submarines and history's first clash between steam-propelled ironclads. Railways and telegraphs – the former used to carry men and supplies, and the latter to coordinate the movements of the armies over vast distances – played a key role. In all these ways the war, far from consisting of 'two mobs chasing each other' (General Helmut von Moltke), actually provided a better foretaste of World War I than did the Wars of German Unification which followed.

Beginning of the Wars of German Unification

<u>1864</u>

The first of the three wars of German Unification was waged by Prussia, led by Otto von Bismarck, and Austria against Denmark. At issue were the provinces of Holstein and Schleswig. The war was decided on 18 April when Prussian troops stormed the fortifications of Düppel, in the south-eastern corner of Jutland. Thereupon Denmark surrendered.

When Prussia and Austria could not agree who would own the two provinces, the former declared war on the latter. By this time Prussia had established a revolutionary system of mobilisation. Making full use of railways and telegraphs, it was able to concentrate its troops with unequalled speed and precision. Following some minor clashes in Bohemia, two Prussian armies, coming from two different directions, caught the Austrians between themselves at Königgrätz. Here the Prussians, thanks in part to the superior rate of fire of their Dreyse breech-loading rifles, prevailed. The defeat left the Austrians practically defenceless. It forced them to sign an armistice under which they agreed to the creation by Prussia of a North German Federation and also surrendered Venice to Italy.

The third war was fought between Prussia and France. This time it was the latter, under Napoleon III, which initiated hostilities in July 1870. Again making full use of their railways, the Prussians invaded France. They surrounded and defeated their opponent's main army at Sedan (where Napoleon

Napoleon III, the loser of Sedan.

himself was taken prisoner) and besieged another large force at Metz, which was ultimately forced to surrender. By early 1871, assisted by their superior cast-steel artillery, they were besieging Paris. Meanwhile the war had spread into the French countryside where remnants of Napoleon's Army and members of the population fought small-scale engagements and waged a guerrilla campaign against the Prussians or Germans. In the end Paris was forced to surrender. This was followed by a vicious civil war as the Germans, watching from Versailles, proclaimed an empire.

The war led to the surrender of Alsace and Lorraine to Germany. It was widely understood as a triumph for the German military system, centring as it did on conscription, reserve service, and the effective use of railways and telegraphs. All these were carefully prepared and coordinated by the Minister of War, Albrecht von Roon, and the Chief of the General Staff, General Helmut von Moltke. With Bismarck's backing, they made the German army into one of the most modern and most powerful in the world. This position it continued to claim until the end of World War II.

70

The Battle of Lissa

<u>1866</u>

Ever since Nelson destroyed Napoleon's fleet at Trafalgar in 1805, naval battles had been extremely rare. Meanwhile, starting in the 1830s, an entirely new type of ship, steam-propelled and with their wooden sides clad with iron, entered service. Thus the Battle of Lissa provided naval observers, constructors and planners with a unique opportunity to form an idea of what future naval warfare might be like – an idea, as it happened, which turned out to be false.

The battle was fought in July as part of the war between Italy and Austria. Sailing up the Adriatic with the objective of capturing Venice, the Italians were preparing to land on the Island of Lissa when their commander, Admiral Carlo di Persano, received news that an Austrian force under Admiral Wilhelm von Tegetthoff was coming for him from the north. On the face of it, Persano had little to worry about. Not only did his ironclads outnumber the Austrian ones twelve to seven, but they included the *Affondatore* (sinker) which, with its revolving turrets, was one of the most modern warships afloat. In terms of the number of guns, the Italians outnumbered the Austrians 641 to 532. Aware of his inferiority, Tegetthoff planned to fight in mêlée, at close quarters. Thanks to Persano's ineptitude, he succeeded.

Sailing north-east, the Italians were able to cross the Austrian T and inflict some damage on their enemies, though no

A late nineteenth-century battleship, complete with ram.

Austrian ships were sunk. Pressing on nevertheless, Tegetthoff, somewhat like Nelson at Trafalgar, found himself between the Italians' lead division and their two rear ones. Making full use of the fact that the Italian rear was out of reach and did not fire a shot throughout the battle, his ships laid about them, trying to ram and being rammed themselves. In this the Austrians proved more effective, sinking two Italian vessels, the *Palestro* and the *Re d'Italia*. Thereupon Persano ordered his remaining ships to retreat.

The victory did not affect the outcome of the struggle: as Prussia defeated Austria, the Austrians were forced to hand over Venice anyway. But it did mislead naval observers the world over into the belief that the ram was the weapon of the future. For some thirty years after Lissa all major warships were equipped with rams. However, the only ship that went to the bottom after being rammed was HMS *Victoria* – which was hit by another British ship, HMS *Camperdown*, during an exercise.

71

Outbreak of the Chinese–Japanese War

Less than thirty years since the so-called 'Meiji Restoration' of 1868, Japan embarked on its first foreign adventure. At issue was control over Korea, 'a dagger aimed at Japan', as one Japanese leader put it, which had long been a tributary state of Beijing. By this time the Japanese navy and army had been modernised, the former along British lines and the latter along Prussian–German ones. By contrast, the Chinese forces were in a deplorable state. One reason for this was corruption, which extended right to the top; some of the funds earmarked for reinforcing the armed forces were actually used to renovate the Summer Palace in Beijing.

The war opened in June 1894 when Beijing dispatched a force of some 2,600 men to assist the Korean government in suppressing a rebellion. In response, Japan sent in a somewhat larger force which it refused to withdraw even after the rebellion had been quashed. The first clash between the two sides took place in July at Asan, just north of Seoul, where the better-armed, better-organised, and better-led Japanese troops forced their opponents to retreat to Pyongyang. On 15 September they captured that city. Two days later the two sides' fleets clashed not far from the mouth of the Yalu River. Eight out of ten Chinese vessels were destroyed, earning Japan near absolute command of the sea.

Gone are the Samurai, long live modern Japanese infantry.

As the Chinese retreated across the river into their own territory, the Japanese followed. The two sides clashed in Manchuria, where several battles took place and resulted in Chinese defeats. Meanwhile the Japanese navy occupied the Pescadores, west of Taiwan, thus isolating the island and preventing the Chinese from reinforcing it. Operating both by sea and by land, other forces invaded the Liaodong Peninsula in southern Manchuria. By March 1895, as Japanese forces approached Beijing, China gave up.

As the war went on, both sides were guilty of massacring wounded men, prisoners of war, and civilians. The Treaty of Shimonoseki, which was signed in April, resulted in Korea moving from the tutelage of China to that of Japan. Having demanded and received an enormous indemnity, paid in silver, the latter also gained Taiwan, the Pescadores, and Liaodong. These Japanese acquisitions opened the door to a clash with Russia, which had its own designs on the area.

72

Spanish–American War

1898

The Spanish–American War had its origins in repeated revolts against Spanish rule in Cuba – revolts that received some American support. They were followed by the mysterious explosion of a visiting American battleship, the *Maine*, in Havana harbour on 15 February 1898. After Spain refused an American ultimatum to surrender Cuba, war ensued.

The first battle took place in Manila Bay on 1 May, when the American commodore George Dewy destroyed the Spanish squadron with hardly any American losses. Having landed, his 11,000 troops were joined by local levies under a veteran freedom fighter, Emilio Aguinaldo. Manila itself fell in August. However, the US had no intention of granting Aguinaldo's demand for Philippine independence. This refusal led to a Philippine uprising against the US that proved considerably bloodier, and much longer, than the war itself.

Meanwhile, on the other side of the world, another American fleet had no more difficulty in disposing of the Spanish one at Santiago, Cuba than Dewey had in Manila Bay. As a result, by July the road to a US invasion of the island was open. Over the next few weeks, some 15,000 American troops landed east of Santiago and set up a base. However, the Spanish troops were

tough, well trained, and armed with modern weapons using smokeless powder. Another obstacle was presented by the difficult terrain.

Worst of all, though, was the problem of yellow fever ('Yellow Jack', as it was known). At one point it rendered no less than three-quarters of the entire American force unfit for service. The antics of Theodore Roosevelt and his Rough Riders notwithstanding, these obstacles prevented the war on land from being fought to a conclusion. Ultimately it was decided by the fact that Spain, following the defeat of its fleets, was no longer able to bring up fresh forces and its resources were exhausted.

This brief, relatively easy, war gave the US all the Spanish colonies outside Africa. It also made the US the dominant power in the Pacific and turned the Caribbean into an American lake. Thus it marked America's emergence as a new Great Power equal, if not superior, to any of the old ones.

This 1904 war resulted from conflicting Russian and Japanese claims over Korea and Manchuria. In particular, Japan could not accept China's decision to lease the ice-free Port Arthur to Russia and the Russian effort to link that city to the Trans-Siberian Railway. Negotiations having led nowhere, on 8 February Japan's navy attacked Port Arthur without a declaration of war, which only followed three hours later.

Early on, the war centred on the Japanese siege of Port Arthur, which lasted ten months. Meanwhile Japanese troops, having crossed to Korea, occupied that country, marched north, and reached the border of Russian-occupied Manchuria. From there they continued north-east, but suffered heavy casualties in their attempts to break through the Russian positions protecting Port Arthur.

In April 1904 the Russian battle fleet tried to break out of Port Arthur. It was, however, met by the Japanese one. The battle was conducted on both sides by modern battleships at a range of some 13km – then the longest in history. The Russians suffered losses and their attempt to break out failed. However, the Japanese on their part were unable to destroy the Russian fleet, most of which withdrew back to port.

In January 1905 Port Arthur fell, opening the way for Japanese armies to advance into Manchuria. In February they met the Russians at Mukden, resulting in a massive battle that involved a

At Tsushima, the Japanese destroyed the Russian fleet.

total of some 500,000 men. Although the Japanese prevailed, they took heavy casualties, almost equal to the Russian ones. Furthermore, with every success they were drawing away from their bases, whereas the Russians fell back closer to their own.

The last act in the great drama was played out on 27–28 May, when the Russian Baltic Fleet, having finally arrived from the other side of the world, was annihilated by the Japanese at the great naval Battle of Tsushima. Thereupon the Tsar, whose country was near bankrupt and whose regime was being threatened by revolution, gave up.

The war represented the first major defeat suffered by any European country at the hands of a non-European one since the end of the seventeenth century. It was also the most modern in history until then, drawing the interest of armed forces all over the world. However, their observers failed to recognise the extreme difficulty, and cost, of overcoming modern field fortifications protected by heavy firepower. Instead, arguing that the problems were due to special 'Manchurian' conditions, they continued to believe in the offensive.

74

Outbreak of World War I

1914

In 1914 none of the European Great Powers wanted a general war. Quite a few, however, were ready to risk a limited one to realise their goals.

The first to open fire were the Austrians, who wanted to punish Serbia for the role it played in the assassination of the heir to the Habsburg throne. This brought in Russia, which brought in Germany, which brought in France, which brought in Belgium, which brought in Britain and its empire. Almost from the beginning it was clear that, in terms of sheer size, this war would overshadow all previous ones and even, especially in terms of equipment, all of them combined.

In September, the German attempt to knock France out of the war was halted on the Marne. From then almost until the end of the conflict, the war in the west was characterised by more or less stationary trench warfare. That warfare was punctuated by enormous battles of attrition which, though causing hundreds of thousands of casualties each, never succeeded in forcing a decision. Once Italy entered the war in May 1915, similar conditions prevailed on that front also. Germany and Austria did much better on the Eastern Front, however. In 1915 they overran Poland, and in 1917–18 they forced Russia, whose government had been overthrown by Lenin's Communists, to sue for peace.

With the Ottoman Empire having joined Germany and Austria, the war spread to Macedonia, the Caucasus, Palestine, and Iraq.

English soldiers on the attack, World War I.

Naval operations also played a key role. Though there were few major actions by surface fleets, the British blockaded Germany whereas the Germans turned to submarines in an attempt to starve out Britain. Both sides also used aircraft – during the war the main belligerents between them produced 250,000 machines. Their missions included reconnaissance, air-to-air combat, close support, interdiction, and, increasingly, 'strategic' bombing of cities and factories.

A critical turning point came in April 1917 when the US, under President Woodrow Wilson, joined Britain and France. In the spring of 1918 Germany, now run by General Erich Ludendorff, made a last determined attempt to break through in the west and knock France out of the war. In this it failed, with the result that, over the next few months, it was overwhelmed by Allied superiority in men and materiel. When the war finally ended in late 1918, four empires (German, Russian, Austrian, and Ottoman) had either been decisively beaten or disintegrated, leaving the US as the strongest power in the world.

75

Outbreak of the Russian Civil War

1917

In November 1917, Lenin's Bolsheviks seized power in Saint Petersburg. Three months later Russia and Germany signed the Peace of Brest-Litovsk under which the former not only surrendered vast territories to the latter but was forced to recognise the independence of the Ukraine. The Treaty freed the Bolsheviks' hands to wage a vicious civil war which only ended in 1922; even so, some rebellions remained to be put down. Participating in the war were dozens of different militias, some ideological, others local, in character. However, the main contenders were the Bolshevik Red Army on one hand and the Whites, supporters of the deposed Tsar, on the other.

The Bolsheviks occupied the centre of the country, St Petersburg and Moscow included. Around them, the war was fought on three main fronts. One was the Baltic Countries where the enemy, consisting of levies under General Nikolai Yudenich, at one point almost took Saint Petersburg. The other two were the Ukraine, where the Bolsheviks faced White forces under General Pyotr Wrangel, and Siberia, where the White commander was Admiral Aleksander Kolchak. In addition the Poles, having regained their independence after over 100 years, took the opportunity to try to reoccupy territories they had lost since the eighteenth century. To top it all, no fewer than eight foreign nations, all hoping to restore the Tsar and/or to seize Russian lands, participated in the war to one extent or another.

Its great brutality apart, what characterised the war was the exceptionally low ratio of troops to the enormous spaces. As had also happened during the American Civil War, this fact made possible some of the last massive cavalry operations in military history under the Red General Semyon Budyonny. Given how bad the road system was, considerable use was made of armoured trains – a Bolshevik specialty that was employed practically nowhere else. Operating on internal lines, the Bolsheviks, through an almost superhuman effort under the overall command of Leon Trotsky, defeated their enemies one by one. The last major front to be cleared was the Siberian one, where Vladivostok fell in October 1922.

The war led to anything between 7 million and 12 million casualties, most of them civilians who perished from hunger, cold and disease as much as due to active military operations. In the east and south, Russia, now known as the Soviet Union, was able to re-establish its previous borders. In the west, though, it lost considerable territories to Poland and the newly established Baltic countries.

76

Outbreak of the Spanish Civil War

1936

The war started when the Spanish Army in Morocco, commanded by General Francisco Franco and supported by various royalist and clerical organisations in Spain itself, revolted against the elected socialist government in Madrid. Colonial troops were flown across the Straits of Gibraltar, enabling them to establish a bridgehead in southern Spain. Other army units, based in Pamplona, Burgos, Zaragoza, Valladolid, Cádiz, Córdoba, and Seville supported the coup. However, attempts to seize other key cities, especially Madrid and Barcelona, failed.

The outcome was a bloody civil war in which Italy and Germany supported the rebels while the Soviet Union supported the government. The latter's forces were joined by volunteers, most of them originating in France and Britain and totalling perhaps 25,000 men, who were known as the International Brigades. By the end of 1936 Franco's Nationalists held western Spain, except for a narrow strip along the Basque coast; the Republicans controlled the east and south-east.

As time went on and both sides organised their forces, the war assumed an increasingly conventional character. It also acted as a laboratory in which both sides, and even more so their foreign sponsors, tested new weapons, organisations and doctrines, especially aircraft and tanks. Important turning points were the Nationalists' occupation of north-western Spain

in early 1937; the successful Republican defence, conducted under the slogan '*No Passaran*' ('they will not pass') of Madrid shortly thereafter; the Battle of Teruel, fought from December 1937 to February 1938, which brought the Nationalists to Spain's south-eastern coast and cut the Republican territory in half; the Nationalists' occupation of Catalonia in early 1939; and finally the fall of Madrid in March of the same year.

An ideologically based conflict if ever one there was, the war was fought with great fanaticism, leading to numerous atrocities on both sides. Long after it was over, Franco's military, police, and security apparatus continued to retaliate against their enemies and suppress them, leading to bitterness that lasted for decades. The total number of dead was around 500,000, with a similar number fleeing the country. Nevertheless, in the popular mind the strongest impression remains that of the northern city of Guernica where, in April 1937, a German bomb attack killed between 200 and 300 people. The attack was immortalised by Pablo Picasso's *Guernica*, widely considered the most influential painting of all time.

77

Outbreak of the Second Chinese- Japanese War

1937

The origins of this war go back at least as far as 1931 when Japan occupied Manchuria. This was followed by a large number of incidents, culminating in July 1937 when Chinese and Japanese troops fought at the Lugou (or Marco Polo) Bridge. A full-scale battle developed, leading to the Japanese occupation of Beijing and its port, Tianjin.

China, governed by General Chiang Kai-shek and his Kuomintang (Nationalist) Party, responded by attacking the Japanese colony in Shanghai. The fighting escalated until the Japanese, using as many as 200,000 troops in the air, at sea, and on land, finally captured the city in November. Yet this was only the beginning as the Japanese both expanded their hold on China's eastern and south-eastern coasts, and advanced inland. In time they even reached Changsha, in Hunan, over 1,000km west of Shanghai. The Chinese Army proved no match for the better organised, better equipped, and utterly ruthless Japanese. The more so because Chiang, even as he was trying to resist them, was also forced to deal with Mao Zedong's Communist Party which was planning to overthrow the Kuomintang and assume power.

The forces on both sides were massive. Japan committed as many as a million men, whereas China raised no fewer than three times that number. Yet there were few major battles. Almost every time the Japanese struck in one direction or another, they were able to gain their objectives. But doing so availed them little: the extent of land and number of people to be subjugated were simply too large for Tokyo to handle. It was made all the more difficult because the Chinese Nationalists were receiving foreign aid, first from the Soviet Union and then, starting in 1942, from the Western Allies in India. And because, from late 1941, Japan was also fighting a world war in the Pacific.

The Chinese waged a vicious guerrilla war, which in turn was countered by even more vicious Japanese repression. Among the means used, or at least tested, were chemical and bacteriological weapons. The struggle, which led to millions of casualties, finally ended in July–August 1945. As the Soviet Union invaded Manchuria, it forced the surrender of the million troops forming the Japanese Kwantung Army. Meanwhile, the government in Tokyo, in the aftermath of the bombing of Hiroshima and Nagasaki, decided to surrender and ordered its remaining troops in China and South-east Asia to do the same.

78

Outbreak of World War II in Europe

1939

World War II was fought in two theatres, Europe and the Pacific, which while linked in some ways were almost entirely separate in many others. That is why, considering also its sheer size, it will be discussed in two parts rather than one.

The war opened with a German invasion of Poland, which in turn brought in the UK and France. Using the most modern available combination of armoured and air forces, the Germans occupied Poland (September 1939), defeated France (May–June 1940), and drove Britain off the European continent. They also picked up Denmark, Norway, and the Benelux countries. However, their attempt to defeat the Royal Air Force and invade the British Isles failed. As in World War I, the outcome was a British blockade of Germany and a German counter-blockade, waged mainly with the aid of submarines, of Britain.

Having failed to subdue Britain, Germany's dictator, Adolf Hitler, hesitated. In the end he decided to attack the Soviet Union in the hope that, once victory there had been achieved, he would be able to confront Britain and the US if necessary. Meanwhile he sent forces to support his ally, Italy, in the Mediterranean. The invasion of the Soviet Union, launched by

3.5 million troops, started in June 1941. It took the Germans to the gates of Moscow, but failed to finally defeat the USSR. After the US entered the war in December 1941, Germany was still able to win some major battles in Russia and North Africa. However – so immensely superior were the forces arrayed against it – the ultimate victory would go to its enemies.

By the end of 1943 the Soviets, led by Joseph Stalin, had regained about two-thirds of their lost territory. Meanwhile, in the Mediterranean, Britain under Winston Churchill and the US under Franklin Roosevelt tightened the ring around Germany. In July Hitler's major ally, Italy, deserted him. Britain and the US, having won the war at sea, also opened a massive bombing campaign of Germany. The June 1944 Anglo-American landing in Normandy forced the latter to engage on a hopeless fight on two fronts even as the Soviets advanced through the Baltic countries, Poland, and the Balkans. On 25 April 1945 Allied troops coming from the east and west finally met on the Elbe. Five days later Hitler committed suicide, leaving a devastated continent behind, the war ending shortly thereafter.

79

Outbreak of World War II in the Pacific

1941

The war in the Pacific started on 7 December 1941 with a massive Japanese, carrier-borne, surprise air attack on the US base at Pearl Harbor. Next, Japanese forces burst out in all directions. Within a few months they had overrun Burma, Thailand, Indochina, Indonesia, Malaysia, Singapore, Hong Kong, and northern New Guinea. In the Pacific, they occupied the Philippines and fortified a protective perimeter of islands that reached thousands of miles north-west, west, and south-west of Tokyo. Throughout this, ground troops were essential for holding or taking fortified positions. However, compared with the European theatre their numbers were small, whereas the role played by air and naval forces was relatively larger.

The Japanese suffered their first major setback at the Battle of the Coral Sea, in May 1942, when American and Australian naval forces prevented them from seizing Port Moresby in New Guinea. This was the first naval engagement in history in which the two sides, using carriers, never sighted one another. A month later a Japanese attempt to capture Midway was repulsed with heavy losses. In both battles signal communications – meaning the interception and decoding of enemy radio transmissions – played a critically important role.

Next, the Allies went on the offensive. Attempts to regain Burma and Thailand by attacking from India only made limited progress, and the appalling terrain – part jungle, part the highest mountain chain on earth – made communication with China

Japanese aircraft over a sunken American battleship, Pearl Harbor, 1941.

difficult. The main American offensive proceeded in two prongs: one, commanded by Admiral Chester Nimitz, moved across the Pacific; the other, commanded by Douglas McArthur, did the same from New Guinea and aimed at the Philippines. Both campaigns hopped from island to island, isolating each one, bombing and shelling it, and landing on it. Japanese resistance was often ferocious, leading to heavy casualties on both sides.

In June 1944 the US Navy, in the Battle of the Marianas, all but terminated what remained of the Imperial Navy. Meanwhile American submarines played havoc with the Japanese merchant fleet until imports, and even trade between the home islands, were all but halted. The final step was the destruction of Japan's cities, Tokyo included, by American heavy bombers. Using incendiaries, they killed hundreds of thousands. On 15 August 1945, having been hit by two atom bombs, the Japanese government surrendered.

The war was the largest in history by far; for instance, three times as many aircraft were produced by the main belligerents than in World War I. The number of those who wore uniform was probably 70–80 million, whereas the number of dead, both military and civilian, is estimated at 60 million.

80

First (and Last) Use of Nuclear Weapons

1945

The first to envisage something like a nuclear weapon was probably the British science-fiction writer H.G. Wells in *The Last War: A World Set Free* (1914). Critically important steps towards building the bomb were the splitting of uranium by Otto Hahn and Lise Meitner in 1939, and the activation of the first self-sustaining chain reaction by Enrico Fermi in 1942. That summer, an industrial-scale effort to develop the bomb, known as the Manhattan Project, got under way at Los Alamos, New Mexico.

The first test was held on 6 July 1945. By that time two other devices, one based on the fission of uranium and the other on that of plutonium, were also approaching completion. On 6 and 9 August they were dropped on Hiroshima and Nagasaki, respectively, killing as many as 200,000 people between them. This figure includes both those who died on the spot and those who were felled by radiation disease over the subsequent months and years.

The first bomb developed a power of some 15,000 tons of TNT, the second as much as 20,000. The testing of the first fusion (also known as hydrogen, or thermonuclear) bomb in 1952 meant that, in theory at any rate, the power of the bomb became unlimited. Early on the bombs were so large that only

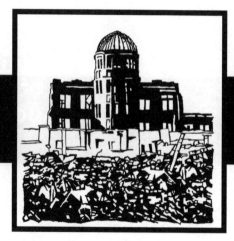

The ruins of Hiroshima.

the heaviest bomber aircraft could deliver them. Later, however, many kinds of aircraft and ballistic missiles, as well as cruise missiles, could do the same. So could artillery shells, bazookas, and, perhaps, suitcases. There was even talk of nuclear mines, though no country is definitely known to have deployed them.

At first only the US had the bomb. In 1949 the Soviet Union tested a device; but only a few other countries followed suit. Currently (2016) just nine out of some 200 countries – in other words, 5 per cent – have them. Each time another country went nuclear fears were expressed that the outcome might be war and apocalypse. Each time deterrence prevailed and the opposite happened. As of 2016, even North Korea had declared it would not be the first to use the bomb. Nuclear proliferation and fear of a nuclear holocaust are almost certainly one reason – indeed the most important reason – why the chances of the average man dying in war are smaller today than they have ever been in history. It is also why, as the next part will explain, war is in full regression.

Part V

THE REGRESSION OF WAR

1945 CE–Present

81

Resumption of the Chinese Civil War

1946

In China, the ruling Kuomintang Party and Mao's Communists had been involved in more or less open conflict since 1927. Japan's war on China and World War II caused this struggle to be pushed into the background; however, no sooner had Japan been defeated than it resumed.

Previously the Communists, based in north-western China, had engaged in guerrilla operations. Following the doctrine laid down by Mao, when the enemy advanced they retreated; when the enemy halted, they advanced; and when the enemy retreated, they pursued and harried. Now, having mobilised no fewer than 3 million troops (1 million regulars, 2 million militia), and in possession of Soviet weapons as well as captured Japanese ones, they went over to conventional warfare. Opposing them were Chiang Kai-shek's American-supplied, -armed, and -supported forces. A large-sale Kuomintang offensive, aimed at wiping out the Communists in 1946–47, failed after bitter and enormously expensive fighting. Turning the table on their opponents, in 1948 the Communists occupied north-eastern China, destroying some of the best Kuomintang armies and capturing vast quantities of American equipment.

From the north-east, the Communists turned their attention to north-central China. With this area in their hands, at the end of 1948 they launched an offensive against Beijing, which fell on 31 January 1949. In the process Kuomintang forces, nominally forming no fewer than 173 divisions, were destroyed, as much by disorganisation and desertion as by active military operations. It remained for the Communists to cross the Yangtze River and pursue their opponents in the south, where they successively took Nanjing, Guangzhou, and Chongqing. When Chiang and the remainder of his troops fled to Taiwan on 10 December, the war was effectively over. All that remained was to reoccupy Tibet as well as some Muslim provinces that had slipped from Beijing's control during the civil war.

The Communist victory, achieved at the cost of almost unimaginable bloodshed on both sides, ended China's 'century of humiliation' which had opened with the Opium War a hundred years earlier. The outcome was to recreate a united China, minus only the city of Hong Kong and the Island of Taiwan. Hong Kong was returned by Britain in 1997. As for Taiwan, it still remains in a sort of limbo between independence and full incorporation.

82 Outbreak of the Indochina War

1946

W orld War II having ended, the French tried to restore their rule over Indochina. Thereupon the native resistance movement, Viet Minh, started guerrilla operations. At peak the French forces, including, besides European troops, colonial units and local allies, numbered over 300,000 men. Most of the fighting took place in North Vietnam, but it also spread into the south and the neighbouring French colonies, Cambodia and Laos.

Having seized control of China in 1949, Mao's Communists started providing large-scale aid to the Viet Minh. As in all such conflicts, the main problem facing the French was how to bring their elusive opponents, who were often able to shelter either among the population or in the jungle, to battle. Their chosen method for doing so was to occupy positions across the Viet Minh's communications with China so as to force the enemy to attack them. Tactically and logistically, the operations were to be supported from the air, where the French enjoyed absolute command. Early on, the strategy seemed to work. First at Hoa Binh in late 1951, then at Na San in late 1952, the Viet Minh under General Võ Nguyên Giáp attacked French strongholds. Twice it was forced to withdraw with heavy casualties.

Encouraged, the French tried to repeat their success at Dien Bien Phu, a remote jungle location. In March 1954 they landed 9,000 men in the area by parachute, set up a so-called

Viet-Minh troops during the First Indochina War.

'hedgehog defence' (a defence pointing in all directions), and started building an airstrip. Eventually the number of French troops who took part reached 15,000. They came under attack by over 60,000 Viet Minh, including entire divisions equipped with heavy artillery, which, in an almost superhuman effort, they had dragged through the jungle. Particularly important were the anti-aircraft defences. Positioned on the hills around Dien Bien Phu, they prevented the French from bringing in supplies and reinforcements.

After two months of fierce fighting, with only a few strongholds still holding out, the French surrendered. It was the greatest defeat inflicted by native troops on European colonial forces in history until then. Dien Bien Phu also entered history as the last large-scale operation involving airborne assault.

The Geneva Peace Conference of July 1954 called for the creation of a united, independent Vietnam and free elections to be held. However, the authorities in South Vietnam, supported by the US, refused to go ahead with the election and the unification, thereby laying the groundwork for the Vietnam War soon to follow.

83

First Round of the Indo-Pak Wars

1947

The background to this war, and to those that followed, was a conflict over Kashmir, which was occupied by India but claimed by Pakistan. Another factor was Pakistan's fear that India, never having reconciled itself to the partition of the subcontinent, would do whatever it could to reunite it.

The first war lasted from October 1947 to January 1949. On both sides it was fought by veterans of Britain's Indian Army, armed with leftover weapons and reinforced by local militias. Accompanied by vast numbers of civilian dead among the population of India, the war proved inconclusive as the fronts froze and a so-called 'Line of Control' separating the two sides was established.

The war over, both sides immediately started building up their armies for the next round. It got under way in the summer of 1965 when Pakistan, its forces provided with American equipment and perhaps in the hope of taking what it could before India built a nuclear bomb, invaded Kashmir. However, India proved too large a nut for a Blitzkrieg to crack. Counter-attacking in the west, its forces occupied some Pakistani territory. In the end, a ceasefire was signed and the *status quo* restored.

The third war was fought in December 1971. The background was formed by an uprising in East Pakistan. It led to harsh Pakistani repression, which drove millions across the border into India, which caused the latter, now under Indira Gandhi, to intervene. Expanding, hostilities took place not just on land and in the air but at sea as well. As the Pakistani Army disintegrated, India invaded West Pakistan, but was forced by American pressure to call a halt. The war ended with the Indians withdrawing and Pakistan losing control of East Pakistan, where the new state of Bangladesh was established.

Both between these rounds and after they had ended, relations between the two countries were punctuated by countless border incidents, skirmishes, and terrorist acts. The largest of these was the so-called Kargil War in 1999, which again ended in a stalemate. Since then both sides have been building up their forces, complete with modern fighter-bombers, naval vessels, ballistic missiles, and cruise missiles. With both in possession of nuclear weapons, though, another large-scale clash appears unlikely.

84

Opening Round in the Arab-Israeli Wars

<u>1948</u>

The 1948 war originated in a dispute between Arabs – not yet known as Palestinians – and Jews as to who owned Palestine. Later it was joined by the armies of Lebanon, Syria, Transjordan, Iraq, and Egypt, which tried to support the Palestinians. Fought on both sides with leftover weapons and, on the Arabs' part, supreme incompetence, the war led to the establishment of Israel as well as the occupation by Jordan of the West Bank and by Egypt of the Gaza Strip.

The next round opened in October 1956 when Israel, France, and Britain attacked Egypt. Israeli forces, much better led than their opponents, overran the Sinai in just six days. Meanwhile French and British troops landed in Port Said in an effort to restore control over the Suez Canal. In the end the allies, largely because of US and Soviet pressure, were forced to withdraw.

In 1967 the Egyptians closed the Straits of Tiran, provoking an Israeli attack. First, a devastating blow by the Israeli Air Force destroyed the Egyptian Air Force on the ground. Next its ground forces, spearheaded by armoured divisions, overran the Sinai and Gaza. When Jordan and Syria joined Egypt, they too came under attack, losing the West Bank (including East Jerusalem) and the Golan Heights respectively.

In October 1973 Syria and Egypt launched a surprise attack on Israel. The war that ensued was both the largest conventional

Israeli soldiers, 1948 style.

one since at least 1953 as well as the technologically most advanced one in history until then. Relying primarily on their armoured divisions and aircraft, the Israelis reconquered the Golan and surrounded part of the Egyptian Army. But they did not succeed in knocking out either of their opponents.

Another war broke out in June 1982 when Israel invaded Lebanon from where terrorists had been attacking it for years. Using some of the most advanced weapons on land, in the air, and at sea, within the week the Israelis forced the Syrians to leave Lebanon and reached Beirut. They did not, however, succeed in overcoming a vicious guerrilla war that only ended when the last Israeli troops left Lebanon in 2000.

These wars formed part of a long chain of hostilities, large and small, that has not yet ended. Operationally the Arabs lost every round. Strategically, though, the Israelis never succeeded in breaking their enemies' will. After 1982 they also discovered that operational success did not necessarily guarantee victory over guerrillas, terrorists, and insurgents.

85

Outbreak of the Korean War

The war opened on 25 June 1950 when North Korean forces, under the supreme command of Kim Il-sung, crossed the border with South Korea. Spearheaded by Soviet-built tanks, and finding their opponents unprepared, they quickly captured Seoul. From there they pushed all the way to Pusan at the tip of the peninsula, which they besieged. However, the US, with some support from its UN allies, brought in forces to reinforce South Korea. In September those forces, commanded by General Douglas McArthur, carried out a daring amphibious landing at Inchon, threatening to cut off the North Koreans and forcing them to withdraw.

Thereafter MacArthur, ignoring Chinese warnings, pushed north up to the river Yalu that marked the border between North Korea and China. Other forces recaptured Seoul. However, MacArthur's gains did not last for long. In October Beijing, sending its own troops to participate in the war, forced him to retreat as fast as he had come. By the end of the year the front was back along the 39th parallel, more or less where it had been where the war had begun.

In April President Harry Truman fired MacArthur and replaced him with General Matthew Ridgeway. A struggle of attrition developed, in which the Chinese, to counter the US advantage in firepower, sent in no fewer than 700,000 troops in so-called 'human wave' attacks. In the process Seoul changed hands two more times, leaving the city in ruins. Intensive fighting also took place in the air. There the Americans, enjoying superiority if not the absolute command they had hoped for, bombed and strafed in an effort to cut off North Korea's communications. When that proved unavailing, they also bombed its cities until they were almost level with the ground.

When the war ended in the summer of 1953 it left the border between the two Koreas practically unchanged. By some accounts peace was brought about by American threats to use nuclear weapons on North Korea and China. However, that story has never been conclusively proved. Since then, with the two sides glaring at each other across the demilitarised zone, countless incidents, some of them quite dangerous, have taken place. They have not, however, led to another war, and one can only hope this will continue to be the case.

Outbreak of the Algerian War of Independence

The official opening of hostilities took place on 1 November 1954 with a series of terrorist attacks. At the same time the Front de Libération Nationale (FLN) read a proclamation on Radio Cairo. At first the French governor, Jacques Soustelle, was inclined to respond by measures aimed at improving the situation of Algeria's population. Soon, however, the army was called in. As so often, repression led to escalation, and escalation to repression, in an ever-growing cycle of violence. By 1957 not a city throughout Algeria was safe against terrorist attacks in the form of bombings and shootings.

In response, the French deployed no fewer than 400,000 troops, excluding 170,000 so-called Harkis (local auxiliaries). Especially prominent were the Foreign Legion and the colonial parachutists – elite units given to unorthodox methods such as torture and forcing Algerian women to wash the troops' underwear in public in order to show that Algerian men were unable to protect them. Using such methods, the French were able to 'win' the Battle of Algiers in 1958. Yet all they achieved was to push the FLN and its military wing, the Armée de Libération Nationale (ALN), back into the countryside where they waged a classic guerrilla war of hit-and-run raids. Weapons and equipment came from Egypt by way of Tunisia and Morocco. The French tried to close both borders by erecting fences along

French parachutists in Algeria.

them and using helicopters to patrol them; however, those measures were never completely successful.

The war also led to massive upheaval in France itself. In 1958 the Fourth Republic fell and was replaced by the Fifth under General (ret.) Charles de Gaulle. Much to the surprise of many, de Gaulle decided to talk to the FLN. To do so he released its leaders who had been captured earlier in the war when their aircraft was hijacked. The outcome was the 1962 Evian Agreement which granted Algeria independence and resulted in the return of some 900,000 French citizens, plus some of the Harkis, from Algeria to France.

Various estimates put the total number of those who died in the struggle at anything between 350,000 and 1.5 million. French military casualties alone numbered 25,600 dead and 65,000 injured. The war convinced most of the old imperialist powers that the days when they could do as they pleased in the so-called Third World were gone. The only ones who failed to learn the lesson were the two Superpowers, with disastrous results to both.

87

Cuban Missile Crisis

<u>1962</u>

The Cuban Missile Crisis is the only non-war to be discussed in these pages. It started on 16 October when the Soviet Union under Nikita Khrushchev, responding to the deployment of American nuclear-capable ballistic missiles in Italy and Anatolia, stationed its own missiles in Cuba. With Congressional elections imminent, this was something US President John Kennedy felt he could not accept. The outcome was a crisis that brought the world as close to a nuclear exchange as it has ever been.

Following much consultation, Kennedy decided to respond by blockading Cuba so as to prevent additional Soviet forces from reaching it. Direct exchanges of letters between the two heads of state, as well as between Khrushchev and Cuban leader Fidel Castro, did not diffuse the crisis. The most dangerous day was 27 October. On that day the Soviets shot down an American reconnaissance plane over Cuba and US Navy ships dropped depth charges on a Soviet submarine equipped with nuclear torpedoes. Only the presence of mind of one of the three senior Soviet officers on board prevented the world from going up, or perhaps down, in a nuclear holocaust.

The next day, the crisis ended. Kennedy promised to lift the blockade and to refrain from invading Cuba. In return, Khrushchev took his missiles out of Cuba. As part of the deal, the US also removed its missiles from Turkey. However, this part of the agreement remained secret, causing most of the world, and many of Khrushchev's own key advisers, to see the crisis as a resounding American victory. Looking back, the most important outcome was the fear and trembling it caused both in the capitals involved and in practically throughout the world. A fear that, thank God many would say, lingers still.

88

The US Enters the Vietnam War

1965

No sooner did the Vietnamese revolt against the French break out than the US got involved. As the French withdrew in 1955, the US became the main protector of the Republic of South Vietnam against terrorism and guerrilla operations launched against it from the North, providing it with supplies, training, and advisers.

At Ap Bac in 1963, the Viet Minh's successor, the Viet Cong, defeated the Army of South Vietnam. Thereupon a US-approved military coup overthrew and killed the head of state, Ngo Dinh Diem. As the situation continued to deteriorate, the US sent more and more troops – a process that accelerated after Lyndon Johnson became president late in 1963. Direct military hostilities between the US and North Vietnam opened in August 1965 when the latter's torpedo boats allegedly attacked an American destroyer. Thereupon Congress authorised the President to repel 'aggression'.

With more US troops arriving, the war fell into four different parts. First there was the anti-guerrilla struggle in South Vietnam. Second was the US bombing of North Vietnam. Third was the bombing of Cambodia (the 'Hồ Chí Minh Trail', after the North Vietnamese leader) as it was offering shelter to North Vietnamese troops crossing into the South; later, in 1970, US forces also invaded Cambodia. And fourth were numerous American special operations inside North Vietnam.

Helicopters in Vietnam – the first helicopter war.

By 1968 there were no fewer than 650,000 US troops in the theatre. Together with the South Vietnamese Army, they outnumbered their opponents three or four to one. The largest battles were fought early in 1968 at Khe Sanh and Huề. Both ended in American victories, and both only served to make the Viet Cong or North Vietnamese forces renew their emphasis on guerrilla warfare. 'Vietnamisation', the policy declared by President Nixon as he took over a year later, did not work either. Two enormous American bombing campaigns, launched in May and December 1972, succeeded in halting North Vietnamese conventional offensives but did nothing to end the war.

The Paris Peace Accords, which were signed in January 1973, allowed the North the right to take over the South 'after a decent interval', as American Secretary of State Henry Kissinger put it. Two years later, the interval ended. The number of US dead was around 55,000, and that of Vietnamese on both sides, including civilians, perhaps 1.5 million. The war also had the distinction of making Vietnam the most bombed country in history. To no avail, as it turned out.

89

Women's Role in the Military Starts Expanding

c. 1970

Until around 1970, women had rarely played an active role in war (as distinct from uprisings, although even in uprisings most women acted in support). Only during World War I did some countries put women into uniform. Yet even then women only filled administrative, logistic, and medical positions not so different from the ones they had been occupying, as camp followers, for centuries if not millennia past. Furthermore, whereas men were drafted, the women were volunteers and could go home whenever they chose. To this day the only country to make women serve against their will is Israel; even there they enjoy some privileges men do not.

The situation in World War II was similar. After 1945 the women were sent home. Though most Western armies retained a few women, this was only so they could act as a framework for mobilising other women in case a major war broke out. In the event, none ever did. Nevertheless, around 1970 the seemingly insatiable demands of the Vietnam War caused the US military to see whether it could use more women. Once women got their foot into the door, they insisted on their right to fill all military

A dubious experiment: women in the military.

occupation specialties (MOS) as well as equal treatment in every other respect. The outcome is that, in the US military as the most powerful of all, they now form about 16 per cent of all personnel.

Unique in the whole of history as it is, the process is fiercely debated. Supporters see it as a great success: proof that women can, and deserve, to do anything as well as men. Opponents – those who dare speak out – argue that it has led to gross discrimination against male soldiers and to a situation where many of them fear being accused of sexual harassment more than they do the enemy. Another effect has been a general perceived 'softening' of the service, which in turn has been alleged to be one of the reasons why, over several decades now, almost every time Western troops are sent to fight non-Western opponents they are defeated.

90

The US Ends Conscription

1973

Conscription, it will be remembered, entered modern life in 1793 in the form of the French *levée en masse*. From 1870 on all major countries used it, although some, notably Britain and the US, did so only in wartime. The first major country to abandon conscription was Britain in 1960. Later, during the Vietnam era, the fact that most troops were draftees added to the sharp divisions within American society and made the war very difficult to wage. This, as well as the draft's own unpopularity, led to Nixon's promise, while still a candidate, to abolish it in favour of an all-volunteer force.

As the fact that most other countries followed the US shows, other factors also played a role in the change. First, in an age when the cost of new weapons and weapon systems rose into the stratosphere, no country any more could afford to maintain the 'mass' or 'industrial' armies of yore. Second, in an age of sophisticated military technology, which demanded long

As conscription was abolished, the old poster regained its relevance.

training periods and expertise, maintaining forces made up of short-term conscripts no longer made sense. Third, and most important, the on-going proliferation of nuclear weapons meant that no major power any more became involved in any large-scale wars in any place close to its own frontiers.

Such being the situation, one country after another followed the American example. A symbolic turning point took place in 1996 when France, the mother country of conscription, followed suit. Equally symbolically, the decision was accompanied by some nuclear tests – as if to say, the fact that France's young men will no longer have to wear uniform does not mean it is unable to wage war in pursuit of its interests.

91

Soviet Invasion of Afghanistan

1979

This war started when the Afghan government, itself installed by a pro-Soviet coup a year earlier, asked for Moscow's help in fighting a rebellion. Thereupon Soviet leader Leonid Brezhnev sent in his own troops, which quickly overran Afghanistan's main population centres. This early Soviet success caused *Newsweek* to praise the Red Army as the most powerful in the whole of history.

As had happened to many other would-be conquerors after 1945 in particular, though, the outcome was not to end the war. Rather, it was to drive it into rural areas, of which Afghanistan has plenty, which provide excellent conditions for guerrilla warfare. The Soviets killed hundreds of thousands of people and drove millions of refugees across the borders. At one point they were even said to have used chemical and biological weapons, though firm proof of this is lacking. Yet results were slow to come. One reason for this was the fact that the US, just like the Soviet Union in respect to Vietnam, was always able to provide the rebels, or Mujahideen as they called themselves, with weapons and equipment by way of Pakistan. Particularly important are said to have been the Stinger anti-aircraft missiles which helped neutralise the Soviets' helicopters as one of their

Stinger anti-aircraft missiles helped defeat the Soviets in Afghanistan.

most important weapon systems of all. However, Soviet military authors have denied this.

Major offensives to defeat the insurgency having failed to lead to permanent results, the Red Army and its associated security organisations focused on holding the cities. Much like the Americans in Vietnam, they tried to avert defeat by setting up an indigenous army to do the ground fighting for them. As with the Americans in Vietnam, they failed. At the end of 1988 the new Soviet leader, Mikhail Gorbachev, decided to end the agony by pulling his forces out of Afghanistan.

The number of Soviet soldiers who died was probably around 15,000. Though this was less than the Soviets sometimes lost in a single day of World War II, the war seemed to do much to undermine confidence in the communist system. In this way it may well have contributed to the demise of the Soviet Union in 1991.

92

Outbreak of the Iran-Iraq War

1980

Following the Islamic Revolution of 1978, Iran was in chaos. This encouraged Iraqi dictator Saddam Hussein to try to overrun some of its south-western, oil-producing, provinces. Apparently he expected the war to last a few weeks. Instead, it lasted eight years.

Saddam's first move, in September 1980, was to try to destroy the Iranian Air Force. In this, however, he failed, enabling the Iranians to strike back at Iraqi targets, both civilian and military, including a nuclear reactor then under construction to the south of Baghdad. Late in the same month the Iraqis succeeded in capturing the city of Khorramshahr, at the mouth of the Gulf. However, the Iranians mobilised both their army and the Revolutionary Guard. By March 1981 the front had frozen, more or less, as both sides settled into trench warfare in many ways reminiscent of World War I.

In late 1981 the Iranians went on the offensive, and in May 1982 they recaptured Khorramshahr. By this time the Iraqi Army was demoralised and Baghdad itself seemed in danger. However, virulent Islamic propaganda issuing from Tehran frightened much of the world, including the US, some European members of NATO, Saudi Arabia, and the Gulf states, into the belief that the Mullahs were bent on exporting their Islamic revolution.

Gas warfare during the Iran–Iraq War.

The outcome was to open the money sluices, and with them the weapon depots, for Hussein and Iraq. Though Hussein was prepared for peace, the Iranians, seeking revenge, refused. Instead they organised human-wave offensives against the Iraqis, which were repulsed, among other things, by the massive use of poison gas.

Meanwhile Iran's international isolation, plus the fall in oil prices that started in 1985, took its toll. Whereas the Iraqis used Saudi and Gulf state money to buy weapons, Iran found it harder and harder to keep the more modern parts of its forces operational. Iraqi air strikes on Iranian ports along the Gulf's eastern shore added to Iran's difficulties. Both sides also launched attacks on tankers in the Gulf, as well as on each other's cities. In the end, after several major Iranian offensives had failed in front of massive Iraqi firepower, the Iranian people tired of the war, whereupon Iran and Iraq agreed on a peace that essentially consisted of a return to the *status quo ante*. But only after perhaps 800,000 men on both sides had died.

93

PTSD Enters the DSM

Post-traumatic stress disorder's entry into the Diagnostic and Statistical Manual of Mental Disorders gained the affliction legitimacy that it previously lacked. The idea that war is bad for the soul and necessarily causes all kinds of psychological complications in warriors is relatively new. In this form, it cannot be found at any time before the American Civil War when it was variously known as Soldiers' Heart or Da Costa Syndrome. The main symptoms were fatigue, shortness of breath, palpitations, and sweating. It was as if patients were suffering from heart attacks, except that, as far as physicians could see, their hearts were fine. Subsequent attempts to explain why the Civil War in particular acted as the turning point in this respect have failed.

During World War I the phenomenon, known as 'nervous disease' (on the German side) or 'shell shock' (on the British one), affected hundreds of thousands of soldiers. Symptoms included extreme fatigue, paralysis, loss of speech and hearing, blindness, uncontrollable trembling, anxiety, stomach contractions, nightmares, bedwetting, impotence and its opposite, priapism, confusion, hysteria, and obsessive-compulsive behaviour. What all the patients had in common was that, as far as anyone could see, they had suffered no organic damage. The fact that many of those who had received damage or suffered from shock did not develop the symptoms added to the mystery.

So widespread has PTSD (Post Traumatic Stress Disorder) become that it has put the effectiveness of many modern armies in question.

World War II repeated this experience. Methods of treatment included rest, sedatives, exercise, and, in severe cases, insulin shock and electric shocks meant to show the patient that his paralyzed limbs could, in fact, be made to function. The importance of social and organisational factors in generating, or preventing, the disease is made clear by the fact that American units suffered proportionally ten times as many casualties as German ones did.

In Vietnam, the phenomenon now known as PTSD which also embraces the inability to reintegrate into civilian life, assumed even larger proportions. Later, in Afghanistan (from 2001) and Iraq (from 2003) things were no better. The point came where returning veterans were obliged to undergo annual tests for PTSD and where anyone who did not contract it came close to being seen as some kind of insensitive brute. The fact that officially recognised patients could draw pensions probably did not help. Currently PTSD, which as far as anyone can see is largely limited to Western armies, has reached the point where several of those armies are hardly capable of going to war at all.

The Iran–Iraq War having ended, most observers expected Saddam Hussein to keep the peace so as to enable his country to recover. Instead, possibly motivated by economic considerations – the price of oil was falling – in the summer of 1990 he occupied Kuwait.

However, Hussein does not seem to have considered the possibility of foreign intervention. Consequently he found himself confronted by a vast coalition made up of the US, several NATO countries, some Far Eastern countries, and some Arab countries. The Soviet Union, which throughout the Cold War had opposed the US at every step, remained aloof. By the end of 1990 both sides had built up their forces. The total number of troops involved in one way or another is said to have been over 1.5 million, of whom 700,000 were American and 650,000 Iraqi. Numbers of aircraft, tanks, armoured personnel carriers, and artillery pieces were in proportion. No wonder Hussein, surveying the array, promised his enemies 'the mother of all battles'.

It did not turn out that way. Right from the beginning, Iraq was cut off from the world by the Coalition's naval forces in the Gulf. Its only ally was Sudan, with which it could only communicate by wireless. After six months during which they built up their forces, on 16–17 January 1991 the Coalition

The Gulf, 1991: the swansong of large-scale conventional war?

launched an air offensive. Using 1,800 aircraft of all types, and proceeding 'inside out', it destroyed most of Hussein's air force on the ground, broke up his ant-aircraft defences, and disrupted his communications. Next it took on his lines of supply and, finally, the forces deployed in and around Kuwait. However, the Coalition did not succeed in destroying Iraq's mobile ballistic missile launchers, which, throughout the war, continued to attack both Saudi Arabia and Israel.

An Iraqi attempt to counter-attack at Khafji was repelled by US and Saudi troops. On 24 February the Coalition launched its ground offensive. The US Marines pressed forward into Kuwait; however, the main move took place much further to the west. There the Coalition forces, commanded by General Norman Schwarzkopf, launched the so-called 'Hail Mary' manoeuvre to outflank the Iraqis. In just 100 hours the Iraqi front collapsed and Kuwait was liberated. However, President George H. Bush brought the war to an end before the Iraqi Army was completely destroyed.

95
The Revolution in Military Affairs (RMA)

c. 1991

No sooner had the Gulf War come to an end than defence experts, officers, and pundits all over the world started trying to evaluate what had happened. In the ensuing debate, a particularly important part was played by four technological developments. They were, 1. the advent and widespread use of precision guided munitions (PGMs); 2. the extensive use of space- air- and land-based sensors for missions such as intelligence, reconnaissance, target selection, and damage assessment; 3. the equally extensive use of computers and data links to coordinate the lot; and 4. the advent of 'information warfare' in an attempt to protect one's own computer networks while disrupting those of the enemy.

Taken together, these developments were said to have led to an RMA comparable to the invention of gunpowder and, during the twentieth century, Blitzkrieg. Supposedly the future belonged to small but highly trained and perfectly equipped armed forces cutting through older ones like knives through butter with only minimal casualties (at the Gulf Iraq may have lost 30–35,000 dead, whereas the number of Coalition troops killed in action was just under 300). Some observers also envisaged something called 'hyper-war' waged by airpower alone, leaving ground forces with nothing better to do than mop up.

Looking back, the pundits seem to have had their way in so far as the Gulf was probably the last 'industrial war'. So

The 'revolution in military affairs' notwithstanding, the role of infantry has not declined.

much smaller have the armies of the most advanced countries become that they would probably not be able to deploy forces half as large they did in 1991. But airpower did not make ground operations superfluous. Nor did high-tech warfare become dominant to the exclusion of everything else.

For this there were two main reasons. First, anyone able to build and maintain forces as sophisticated as those used (on both sides) on the Gulf should also be able to acquire nuclear weapons. With them would come all the proven inhibiting effects such weapons have had on large-scale conventional weapons from 1945 on. Second, countries, people, and groups unable to face modern conventional firepower have increasingly turned to terrorism, guerrilla, insurgency, and sub-conventional warfare (take your pick). In such warfare, as the future was to prove, the role of ground forces, infantry in particular, remained at least as great as it had always been, whereas the advantage of high-tech armies over their enemies was by no means guaranteed.

96

Outbreak of the War(s) in Yugoslavia

<u>1991</u>

Starting in 1945 Yugoslavia, made up of no fewer than seven former Austrian–Hungarian and Ottoman provinces with somewhat different religions and languages, had been governed by a communist dictatorship under Josip Tito. With central rule weakening after Tito's death in 1980, several of those used the opportunity to declare independence from the dominant province, Serbia, and its capital, Belgrade.

The first provinces to break away were Slovenia and Croatia. Slovenia was allowed to go after some shooting that only lasted ten days. However, there was considerable fighting between Croat and Serb forces. In the end, in 1995, the Croats were able to reoccupy all the territory the Serbs had captured early in the war and expel the estimated 250,000 Serb inhabitants of Krajina.

The heaviest fighting took place in Bosnia–Herzegovina. There the Serb minority, strongly supported by Serb leader Slobodan Milošević and determined not to come under Muslim rule, mounted an all-out offensive and engaged in large-scale ethnic cleansing. The most prominent features of the war were the prolonged Serb siege of Sarajevo and the massacre at Srebrenica. Mixed up in it were all kinds of local warlords. Between former communist bosses and simple criminals, they armed their militias with whatever weapons they could find and turned the province into a hell on earth. The war ended in 1995 when Serbia, bankrupt and coming under heavy international

Slobodan Milošević tried to keep his country intact – and paid the price.

pressure, stopped supporting the Serb militias and NATO aircraft bombed them.

The death toll may have amounted to 200,000 people. Much of the world saw the Serb effort to protect first the integrity of the country and then the Serb minority in Bosnia as criminal. Its leaders chose to blame the Serbs, even though in fact all sides were equally guilty of atrocities. That is why, when Milošević launched a campaign to eradicate Muslim terrorists in Kosovo, NATO started bombing Serbia. Thereupon Milošević opened another campaign, this time aimed at driving the Muslim population of Kosovo into Albania. For seventy-eight days the Serbs, with all of thirty-five modern fighter aircraft, held out against NATO's thousand. Until they were overwhelmed.

The Kosovo War enabled the last remaining non-Serb provinces to emancipate themselves from Belgrade's rule. Milošević himself was arrested and died in prison while on trial at the International Criminal Tribunal at The Hague; whereas Hillary Clinton, for helping Kosovo to assert itself against Serbia, later had a statue in her likeness erected by the grateful people of that province.

Strictly speaking, Nine-Eleven – after the date, 11 September, on which it took place – was not a war but an act of terrorism. It was the largest of all, claiming some 3,000 dead. However, it also formed a landmark in military history. It convinced many people that terrorism, not large-scale conventional warfare as the proponents of the RMA had claimed, was the wave of the future.

Behind the day's events stood Al-Qaeda, one of numerous more or less radical Islamic groups with roots in Saudi Arabia and supporters in many countries. How strong those roots were, and how deeply involved some figures in the Saudi government were in organising the bombings, is still not clear. Some of the perpetrators were veterans of the struggles in Afghanistan and Bosnia. Others had been studying in the West, especially Germany. First they hijacked two American civil aircraft, fully loaded with fuel and passengers, and smashed them into the twin towers of the World Trade Center in south Manhattan. A third aircraft hit the Pentagon, while the fourth was aimed at the White House but crashed in Pennsylvania when the passengers struggled with the hijackers.

Magnifying the impact, much of what went on was videotaped and shown on television, worldwide, either in real time or in

something very near it. In most of the West, the outcome was a shudder of horror and a wave of sympathy for the US. Not so in many Muslin countries, however, where there were quite some who identified with the bombers.

The immediate outcome of the attacks was to make practically all countries sink vast resources into beefing up security. There followed President George W. Bush's declaration of a 'global war on terror': an all-out offensive aimed at destroying Al-Qaeda and similar organisations all over the world. In 2001, this 'war' led directly to the US invasion of Afghanistan.

At the time of writing, in mid-2016, the on-going 'war' had registered some successes, including, most spectacularly, the killing in 2011 of Al-Qaeda chief Osama bin Laden by American commandos. However, it is far from won; if, indeed, there is any sense in which it can be 'won' at all. As events such as those that took place in Paris in November 2015 proved, major terrorist attacks remain possible at almost any place, at any time.

98

American Invasion of Afghanistan

2001

P rior to going on the offensive, the US government demanded that the Taliban, who were ruling Afghanistan, extradite bin Laden. This demand having been refused, the US went to war.

After several months of preparation, diplomatic and logistic, the war got under way on 7 October with a spectacular bombardment of the Afghan capital, Kabul. Other Taliban targets all over the country were also hit. This was followed by a ground offensive by the so-called Northern League, a loose coalition of tribal chiefs. Having received suitcases full of dollars, they allowed their men to be led to their objectives by US Special Forces personnel. Among their more interesting antics was a cavalry charge aimed at the city of Mazar-i-Sharif, in the northern part of the country, and its capture.

The Americans and their Afghan allies had little difficulty in capturing the main population centres. However, the US, caught in its own theories concerning the nature and implications of the RMA, hardly had any number of 'boots on the ground'. Consequently the main result of the bombing, though it did kill some Taliban, was to make them run in all directions. Among those who succeeded in doing so, allegedly by giving his cell phone to his driver, was bin Laden himself.

Starting gradually, hostilities developed into full-scale guerrilla warfare. This caused the US and its allies, most of

Afghanistan: the futile war.

them belonging to NATO, to send in reinforcements until, at its peak in 2008–09, they had about 100,000 troops in the country. Even so, the American commander, General Stanley McChrystal, estimated that putting down the insurgency would take 500,000 men five years. But landlocked Afghanistan was not Vietnam. Unlike the latter, it could be reached only by air and by land (by way of Pakistan), making the campaign more costly than it would otherwise have been.

Under these conditions, the only possible 'solution' was to build an Afghan government, raise an Afghan army, equip it, train it, and send it to fight the guerrillas. Attempts to do all this, costing billions and billions of dollars, were made; but without success. At the end of 2014 the Coalition forces, having suffered perhaps 2,500–3,000 dead, officially ended combat operations. The country they left behind mourned an estimated 170,000 dead. All to absolutely no avail, as far as anyone can see.

99

American Invasion of Iraq

2003

When the idea was first floated President Hosni Mubarak of Egypt told his long-time American allies that the outcome of a war in Iraq would be 'to open the gates of hell'. However, the Bush administration was determined to go ahead. It went so far as to manufacture evidence concerning Hussein's ties with terrorism and his continued possession of chemical weapons – weapons that were never found.

Iraq's defeat in the First Gulf War was followed by a decade of sanctions. As a result, it took the Americans and their allies, fielding a force only one-third as large as the one they had used in 1991, just three weeks to reach Baghdad. The number of casualties (on both sides) was also much smaller. However, Hussein's fall and eventual capture and execution proved to be the beginning of the campaign, not its end.

Though elections were held, a government capable of establishing its authority over the whole of Iraq proved impossible to build. The country was positively brimming with leftover weapons, as well as embittered former military personnel able and willing to use them. Under such circumstances a vicious war of all against all – Sunni militias, Shiite militias, breakaway Kurds, criminal gangs, whatever – was inevitable. So, too, was an equally vicious terrorist and guerrilla campaign against the occupying troops. As they had done in

Saddam Hussein was toppled, but the war in Iraq goes on.

Vietnam, the Americans and their allies responded by bringing in more troops until, at peak in 2007–08, they had about 180,000 of them. There were, at the time, some local successes; yet it was clear that, for anything like permanent results to be achieved, a much larger military presence would be needed for a long time to come.

The war cost the US and its allies well over 4,000 dead as well as tens of thousands of wounded, many very seriously. The number of Iraqis who died, mainly after the capture of Baghdad and at the hands of each other, is in the hundreds of thousands and still growing. As domestic opposition to the war grew, President Barack Obama decided to withdraw. Again there was talk of 'Iraqisation', and of the Americans training a new Iraqi army – as if the Iraqis, whose experience with repression was and is second to none, needed democratically minded GIs to teach them how to do it. Most foreign troops were withdrawn in 2011, leaving the country to the depredations of the most vicious terrorist group of all, known as Daesh or ISIS.

100
Outbreak of the 'Arab Spring' Wars

2010

When a revolt toppled the despotic government of Tunisia in December 2010 much of the world applauded. When the revolts spread to Libya, Egypt, and Syria there was talk about an 'Arab Spring'. Hopefully it would resemble the events of 1848 in Europe; which, in the long run, led the continent towards democracy.

It was not to be. True, Tunisia itself, as well as Egypt, escaped the worst violence. The former got a more or less democratic regime, albeit one that is not free of terrorism. The latter held one free election – the only one in 6,000 years of history. But no sooner had it been won by the Muslim Brotherhood than the army took over, restoring the dictatorship.

In Libya, a revolt broke out in February 2011. Had not the US, France, Britain, and some other NATO countries sent their air forces to intervene, dictator Muammar Gaddafi might have crushed it. As things unfolded, his army disintegrated and he himself was killed. The outcome was civil war among various Libyan tribal groups which, six years later, was still going on. Not only did it turn the country into a hopeless mess, but it also offered plenty of scope for terrorist organisations, including both Al-Qaeda and Daesh, to get involved, which Gaddafi had long held at arm's length.

In May 2011 Syrian dictator Bashar al-Assad faced a similar revolt. Some of the groups were allegedly democratic and

Libya's Gaddafi was killed, but the Arab Spring faltered

liberal, others Islamic. Along with Assad's own army, they turned Syria into a flaming, screaming inferno. Again foreign countries and organisations took a hand. Prominent among them were Saudi Arabia, which financed Assad's enemies; Iran, which supported him; Lebanon's Hezbollah (the same); Russia, which fought Assad's 'liberal' enemies; the US and some of its allies, which bombed his Islamic ones; Turkey, which bombed the Kurds; and Israel, which launched occasional air strikes against Hezbollah. The war also merged with the one in Iraq where government forces, supported by the US, were trying to prevent Daesh from setting up a Caliphate.

All these conflicts were fought by relatively small forces on all sides. Nor did the various Arab armies and militias use much high technology; for example, the Syrian Air Force specialised in using helicopters to drop barrels full of explosives on crowded markets. Nevertheless, in Syria alone 500,000 people are said to have died, with no end in sight. *Warre*, it seems, war in its most elemental, Hobbesian sense, has reasserted itself.

Further Reading

Part I

Hamblin, W.J., *Warfare in the Ancient Near East to 1500 BC*, London, Routledge, 2006.

Keeley, L.H., *War Before Civilization*, New York, Oxford University Press, 1996.

Kelly, C., *Warless Societies and the Origins of War*, Ann Arbor, University of Michigan Press, 2000.

Lee, A.D., *War in Late Antiquity*, Oxford, Blackwell, 2007.

Roth, J.P., *Roman Warfare*, Cambridge, Cambridge University Press, 2009.

Sawyer, R.D., *Ancient Chinese Warfare*, New York, Basic Books, 2011.

van Wees, H., *Greek Warfare*, Bristol, Bristol Classical Press, 2004.

Part II

Contamine, P., *War in the Middle Ages*, Oxford, Blackwell, 1986.

Graff, D.A., *Medieval Chinese Warfare*, London, Routledge, 2002.

Kennedy, H., *The Armies of the Caliphs*, London, Routledge, 2001.

Luttwak, E., *The Grand Strategy of the Byzantine Empire*, Cambridge, Belknap Press, 2009.

Nicholson, H., *Medieval Warfare*, London, Palgrave, 2004.

Saunders, J.J., *The History of the Mongol Conquests*, Philadelphia, University of Pennsylvania Press, 2001.

Part III

Bell, D.A., *The First Total War*, New York, Houghton Mifflin, 2007.

Black, J., *War in the World: A Comparative History, 1450–1700*, London, Palgrave, 2011.

Black, J., *Warfare in the Eighteenth Century*, London, Cassell, 1999.

Chase, K., *Firearms: A Global History to 1700*, Cambridge, Cambridge University Press, 2003.

Cipolla, C.M., *Guns, Sails and Empires: Technological Innovation and the Early Phases of European Expansion, 1400–1700*, New York, Pantheon, 1966.

Ferling, J., *Whirlwind: The American Revolution and the War that Won It*, London, Bloomsbury, 2015.

Lambert, A., *War at Sea in the Age of Sail*, London, Cassell, 2000.

Parker, G., *The Military Revolution: Military Innovation and the Rise of the West, 1500–1800*, Cambridge, Cambridge University Press, 1996.

Part IV

Black, J., *War in the Nineteenth Century, 1800–1914*, Oxford, Polity, 2009.

Hastings, M., *All Hell Let Loose: The World at War, 1939–1945*, New York, Harper, 2011.

Headrick, R.D., *The Tools of Empire: Technology and European Imperialism in the Nineteenth Century*, Oxford, Oxford University Press, 1981.

Keegan, J., *The First World War*, New York, Knopf, 1998.

McElwee, W., *The Art of War: Waterloo to Mons,* London, Weidenfeld & Nicolson, 1974.

McPherson, J., *Battle Cry of Freedom: The Civil War Era*, Oxford, Oxford University Press, 2003.

Murray, W., & Millett, A.R. (eds), *Military Innovation in the Interwar Period*, New York, Cambridge University Press, 1996.

Part V

Black, J., *War Since 1945*, London, Reaktion, 2005.
Kaldor, M., *New and Old Wars: Organized Violence in a Global Era*, Stanford, Stanford University Press, 2012.
Mahnken, T.G., *Technology and the American Way of War Since 1945*, New York, Columbia University Press, 2001.
Smith, R., *The Utility of Force: The Art of War in the Modern World*, London, Allen Lane, 2005.
van Creveld, M., *The Transformation of War*, New York, Free Press, 1991.